A SPIRITUAL PRIMER

Hector Esponda

RADHA SOAMI SATSANG BEAS

Published by:
J. C. Sethi, Secretary
Radha Soami Satsang Beas
Dera Baba Jaimal Singh
Punjab 143 204, India

We acknowledge with thanks the permission given
by Brian Hines and Threshold Press to quote material
from *God's Whisper, Creation's Thunder*

Fourth edition 2001

16 15 14 13 12 11 10 09   8 7 6 5 4 3

ISBN 978-81-8256-146-5

Printed in India by: Lakshmi Offset Printers

Table of Contents

Our Current Situation

Who wouldn't like to be happy? The desire for happiness is one of the most powerful fuels that drive human life. Yet how many people could say they ever really achieve it? Is it not a fact that most people spend most of their lives pursuing happiness in one way or another? And they want their happiness to last. They search for it in many ways—in relationships, careers, making money, having sex, reading books, going to the movies, consuming alcohol, taking drugs, going out to eat, going shopping, buying clothes, and in seeking power, popularity or fame. Basically all these things lie outside the person, which implies that happiness is thought to be found through the outside world.

Sometimes, for a brief interlude, a person may feel he has achieved what he was looking for, but then the next moment that feeling is gone. If some sense of satisfaction is experienced through outside things, it never lasts long—and that's the problem. Sooner or later something else is needed. A new source of happiness has to be sought. The mind tires of what it has, and once again the person becomes frustrated or feels that something is lacking. Once more he or she goes out into the world looking for something new. If it is a new car that brings delight, then after a year the delight wears thin and the car becomes just an old model that does not satisfy any longer. It is the same with relationships, the same with careers, the same with entertainment, the same with everything money can buy and with all the so-called thrills of life.

Now, a person may ask, "In this world, is there any joy and happiness that doesn't change and that will remain with me all the time?" Something inside may say, "Yes, such happiness is possible if only things were different...if only I got that promotion...if only I would lose twenty pounds...if only I could find the right person." But then, the world doesn't conform to what we want, and back we climb onto the same old platform of discontent.

So the next question one has to ask is, "Is it possible we are going about looking for happiness in the wrong place?" And to answer this, one needs to answer another question first, "Who or what am I?"

If we took a lion and put it in a cage in the circus, could we get any idea of the animal's real potential? If we took a freshwater fish and put it in the sea, do we think that the fish would survive? The lion would feel imprisoned and suffer; the fish would surely die. This is because each creature, by its very nature, has specific needs. What are our needs as humans? Do we know our own nature? Only if we understand who or what we are, can we know what will satisfy us. Is it possible that we are mistaken as to our real nature? Is this perhaps why we find it impossible to stay happy for long?

A spiritual worldview

Since the human body is constituted of matter, human beings have a physical dimension; but they also have a mental, emotional and spiritual dimension. In order to realize what they are and to experience their full potential, they need to develop all four dimensions. These four aspects of being human may be compared to the four tyres on a car. If one of the tyres is flat, the car does not function properly. Most people dedicate a lot of time and energy to developing their physical, mental and emotional nature. Often they develop one at the cost of the other two. But very few people have any inkling of their great spiritual potential. In fact, many have no idea this exists at all. Consequently, their life lacks balance just like the car with a flat tyre.

The secret to a meaningful and harmonious life is to develop this spiritual dimension. But to do this we need to reorient ourselves. This new orientation towards spirituality will give us a new perspective, the spiritual perspective. It will affect the way we respond to the world. It will help us redefine the way we approach daily life, redefine our values and priorities; and by doing so, it will provide us with a truer picture of who and what we are. With a spiritual worldview, we will better understand our nature and its great potential. This understanding will offer us the key to a deeper and more constant happiness by opening the door to a more balanced and complete life. As the fish needs fresh water to live, and the lion needs the wilderness to thrive, so human beings need spiritual food and spiritual life to feel well and to develop their full potential. The key to happiness lies in bringing spirituality back into our lives. The secret to a happy, carefree and fulfilled life is to make spiritual growth our first priority.

The objects of desire

The main difficulty we face in recognizing our spiritual need is that we are too engrossed in the world and its objects. Our mind has no time or space in its daily agenda to consider anything else. Like a cork cast out on the ocean, the mind rides on one wave of sense impressions after another. Like a monkey, it is never still. The mind is completely absorbed in everything it experiences outside itself. Its every pore is full to the brim with sense pleasures. It is bombarded with dreams and possibilities, saturated with the promises of the world.

The never-ending mental activity of our self-centred egos is reflected in our engrossment with what we think of as ours—our family, friends, career and possessions. But what if none of this truly belongs to us? We know that when we die none of this goes with us. Everyone knows that nothing from this world has ever accompanied a person beyond death, nor can it ever do so. We all know that eventually we have to leave our bodies. We leave behind all the treasures we have accumulated. We say goodbye to our loved ones. Whether we like it or not, everything that concerns the physical world has to be surrendered at death.

In theory, we know all this. But is it also possible that when death comes we will clearly see that we have been deluded, that what we thought was real was just a shadow of reality? Is it possible we will realize that life is something more than what we have just been through?

Building castles in the air

Imagine, as Shakespeare said, the world is a stage. We all come here to play certain roles—as husband or wife, as son or daughter, as creditor or debtor. After our part is played, we make our exit just as actors do in a play and revert to being who we 'really' are. The world, like theatre, is not permanent. If we develop a worldview that puts life in its correct perspective and gives the things of life their proper value, that perspective will also give us the strength to keep from drowning in life's storms. With it we will learn to be in the world without getting pulled down by it. A boat floats on water, but water must not be allowed to get into the boat. If it does, the boat will sink.

Have we ever thought to ourselves how extraordinary it is that we work day and night throughout our lives to possess things that can never be truly ours? We exhaust ourselves running after illusions. Parents, spouse, children, friends, wealth and possessions all disappear at death, and sometimes before we die. With our last breath they are gone forever, yet, throughout our days, we live and work only for them. We discover too late that we have spent our lives building castles in the air.

Pushing and shoving

For many people, much of life consists of trying to keep a balance, as though they were fighting to keep on their feet amidst a vast crowd of people who are pushing and shoving them around. It seems that life demands we become professional jugglers. We want to do our jobs well; to bring up our children well; to romance our loved ones; to spend time with friends, time with our family and time with ourselves. In this complicated way of life that we have created, we also want to take care of our homes, our cars, our bodies, our heads, our hearts, our souls. We also want to play sports, enjoy hobbies, and nurture outside interests. We want all of this, and as if this weren't enough, to complicate matters further, on top of it all we want more money, more power, more recognition, more possessions, more everything. The trouble is we can't have it. And we can't have it all for the simple reason that we don't have the time. Even if we did, once we fulfil one desire, another one creeps up, and our limited amount of time and energy doesn't match with the demands of our desires. No matter how hard we try, we simply are not able, in the time at our disposal, to satisfy all the demands our desires make on our minds.

Balancing our act

To make our lives meaningful, we have to be clear about what is valuable to us. We have to take a good look at our priorities. We are striving for balance; but balance, like other admirable traits, is hard to achieve. Balance means recognizing, out of our many interests, what our real needs are, and then rearranging our priorities to reflect those needs. This usually involves letting go of some of our tightly held pursuits and attachments, and for this we have to be prepared to ask ourselves some tough questions. But it is worth asking them because balance is essential to achieving self-realization, and without knowing who we are, we cannot go very far in life.

Our contemporary society tells us that having balance is about having a spouse, a couple of children, a house, one or two cars, a good job and some hobbies, and being involved with our places of worship and civic activities, and, at the same time, keeping physically fit. The list goes on. True balance has little to do with all these things because they are all *outside* us, and true balance is a state *within*. Balancing the externals of life is fine for someone who is content with life at the surface. But for those who are given to a little reflection, this is not enough. They want to be free from their limitations, free from being owned by their possessions, free from the craziness, disappointments and frustrations of life at this level. They are interested in waking up to what life really is, not in creating more illusions.

Only if we wake up will we know what it means to be alive. For the most part, we don't live; we just exist. Consider that in the meagre lifetime we have been allotted, according to recent statistics we will spend six months at traffic lights waiting for them to change, one year looking through desk clutter for things we have misplaced, two years calling people who aren't in or whose lines are busy, five years waiting in lines and three more sitting in meetings. That's a lot of time being drained away from us. It is not just time we are running out of—it is also the opportunity to make the best of our lives, to experience who we are and know what we really want.

How we spend our time and what we do with it is very important. We complicate our own lives because we mistakenly believe that to be happy and to lead a balanced life we need all these outside things. But it need not be that way. There are other options. To find these options we need to look inwards instead. We need to look within ourselves.

It is the constant pursuit of worldly things and our preoccupation with objects, people and activities that keep us in a circle of suffering and unhappiness. Developing an inner spiritual life is a powerful tool that can help us establish, within ourselves, the balance and the happiness we keep trying to achieve outside. But how does one do this, one may well ask oneself. And the logical answer is, first and foremost, to take the help of those who have successfully addressed the question. We need to be in touch with people who have themselves developed their spiritual potential and can teach us how to do the same.

The mystics

The mystics and saints of the world can teach us how to find precisely what we are looking for because they themselves have attained it. They are living examples of that state of balance we seek.

The term 'mystic' has been very much misunderstood in Western culture. Mystics are often thought of as being aloof, impractical, devoid of common sense, and withdrawn from family life and worldly affairs. However, if we have the good fortune to meet a real mystic, we will see a very different picture. We will see that true mystics do not shun worldly responsibilities. They have, on the contrary, an extraordinarily high level of productivity and efficiency in whatever they do. They are in control of their emotions, thoughts and actions, and they radiate immense peace and joy from within themselves.

The terms 'mystic', 'saint' and 'spiritual teacher', as used throughout this book, refer to someone who has experienced for himself the totality of the universe, has merged with it and has known its every aspect. A true mystic or saint is someone who has authority to speak, from personal experience, about such issues as life and death. Mystics, therefore, can explain to us how to make our lives more meaningful. They can guide us as to which course of action is beneficial for us and which is not.

Because the mystics have first-hand knowledge of the mysteries of the universe, they can answer such questions as these: What happens to us when we die? Where do we come from? How can we rise above our limitations? What is the purpose of life? Does God exist? Is there a soul? How can we find the inner peace and happiness that will put to an end, once and for all, to the pain, boredom, restlessness, loneliness and all the other negative emotions we may face?

The answers to all these questions constitute the ageless *teachings of the saints* and forms the central theme of this book. The teachings of the saints are based on their inner experiences, not on what they have read or heard. Saints are people who have made spirituality the focus of their lives. Living with this focus, they embody the finest human qualities and have transcended normal human limitations. Through a specific technique, they are able to leave their body and return to it at will. They have conquered death and unveiled the mysteries of the universe. Such true mystics or saints have always been present on earth.

Saints and mystics come to this world as spiritual teachers to remind us of who we really are. They come to help us rise above our limitations and see life in its positive totality. They instruct us not to take their words at face value but to prove the truth of their teachings—each one of us, for ourselves—by putting them into practice.

Mystics explain that although we are in a body, we are not a mere body. We are an intricate blending of body, mind and soul, with soul being our essence, the mind its covering, and the body a temporary abode. When the body dies, the soul continues to exist. In other words, death is not the end of our life. Our life continues after our body dies. They tell us that, in fact, there are many dimensions through which the soul can pass, and that this universe, with all its planets, stars and galaxies, is only a tiny portion of the vast ocean of creation. They also tell us that where there is a creation, there is a Creator.

In discussions of the creation of the universe, science has predominantly supported the 'big bang' theory. It is a popular belief that scientists do not admit the existence of God. Therefore some may find it surprising that Albert Einstein—with all his scientific genius and expertise regarding the physics of the universe—concluded that God must exist. He said: "It is enough for me to contemplate the mystery of conscious life perpetuating itself through all eternity; to reflect upon the marvellous structure of the universe, which we can dimly perceive and to try humbly to comprehend even an infinitesimal part of the intelligence manifested in nature." In response to this, Robert Millikan, dean of American Scientists, declared to the American Physical Society: "That is as good a definition of God as I need."

Coming from Einstein, the most eminent scientist of the twentieth century, this very striking and important statement would convince most of us about the omnipresence of the Creator if we only pondered the profound meaning of his words: "It is *enough* for me to *contemplate* the mystery of conscious life perpetuating itself through all eternity; ...to *reflect* upon the marvelous *structure* of the universe, which we can *dimly* perceive and to try *humbly* to comprehend...the *intelligence manifested* in nature."

Historically, people have often insisted that science and spirituality are mutually exclusive, but that is not the case. The writings of scientists like Einstein show that they 'knew' there was something beyond the realm of time and space. However, they were unable to elaborate on it further. Mystics, on the other hand, are scientists of the spirit. They have developed themselves to their full potential and, having mastered the science of the soul, have personally experienced the realms that exist beyond mind and matter. They are, therefore, the best qualified to instruct others as to how they too can develop their full potential.

The Consequences of Our Actions

Saints tell us that, to improve our current situation, first we need to identify what thoughts and actions will lead us to a state of peace and harmony. Desires direct our thoughts, and thoughts govern our actions. Before we do anything, there is a desire, an intention or an urge in our minds. First desire is formed in the mind, then the mind dwells on it, and at some point the mind may be compelled to act.

Actions play a great part in moulding what we are. We act through the physical body, but actions are the outcome of thoughts. Positive or negative actions are the results of positive or negative thinking. Thoughts are the keynotes of our success or failure. It is our thoughts that form our attitudes, and it is our attitudes that determine whether we are happy or unhappy. Attitudes are more important than circumstances, failures or successes, than money or poverty, illness or health. If we have a positive attitude, we will make the best out of even the worst conditions. If we have a negative attitude, we will be miserable even in the best of circumstances. Happiness or unhappiness in life, therefore, is an outcome of how we react. Indeed, our life is shaped by how we react to it. The final consequence of positive actions is happiness, never pain. The final consequence of negative actions is pain, never happiness.

The mind functions like a computer—whatever is the input, that determines the output. First of all, impressions are registered on our mind. Then, by dwelling on these impressions, we make grooves on our mind. These grooves become so deep that we become programmed by them and are then compelled to react according to our own programming. This is why we need to be very careful of what we think. We should keep careful watch over our thoughts and try to dwell upon only those thoughts which will help us develop the right attitude, and which will lead us to do actions that are for our good.

The boomerang effect

Mystics tell us that for every action there is a reaction even though we do not necessarily experience the result immediately. For instance, when one gets drunk, one may experience a hangover the next day. However, the effects of the action of drinking do not necessarily stop at the hangover. Depending on what the person does while under the influence of alcohol, he or she could suffer terrible consequences and even end up in jail or dead. The same principle applies to a positive action. A person who adopts a healthier diet or exercise programme may not immediately feel the benefits but can be assured of positive results sometime in the future.

Whether it is a good or a bad action, once we have taken it, it is bound to transform into a result. The consequences will descend upon us, just as once thrown, a boomerang will come right back at us. The greater the force we apply to throwing a boomerang, the greater the force with which it comes back. This is an objective law, not an emotional or subjective judgement.

Newton, in his third law of motion, expressed the principle that for every action there is an equal and opposite reaction. In science this law is painstakingly exact, and not even a microscopic electron can move without creating an effect. This is the law of action and reaction. Just as it applies to physics, so it also applies to us as the law of cause and effect, or karma (a Sanskrit word that literally means action). This law of action and reaction that governs our universe as well as ourselves explains why some people are miserable while others are happy, why some are poor while others are rich. Through the understanding of this law we can comprehend many of the so called injustices of the world.

What happens to us is the direct result of our actions. There are no exceptions. We cannot avoid this law. We are responsible for our actions, and it is we who have to deal with their consequences.

Saints tell us that the ocean of actions we have done in the past is unfathomable. It is so vast, and there is such a backlog of pending dues—of consequences to be worked through—that it is almost impossible for us ever to work them through. When we come in contact with a living saint or a true spiritual teacher and start to follow his advice, we begin to comprehend how much our past actions have shaped our current situation and how they even account for what we love and what we hate. We thus learn to accept responsibility for our actions of the past and react less strongly when faced, today, with their consequences. By doing spiritual practice, we gradually untie the knots that bind us to our past actions. We become capable of controlling our reactions and we avoid negative actions that might further complicate our life in the future.

What Happens at the Time of Death

According to the saints, our actions are so important that the manner and time of our death is determined by their sum total. In the book *The Path of the Masters*, Dr Julian Johnson writes at length on the implications of the law of action and reaction for death and for life. Paraphrasing part of his discussion on karma, we start with the self-evident fact that everyone has to die some day. Whether man or beast, rich or poor, healthy or diseased, nobody escapes death. All have to pass through its gate. The soul that has taken the physical form has to discard it. We all know that we have to quit this world some day, but we do not know when.

When a person dies, the soul current begins to withdraw from the body, starting with the soles of the feet and ending with the top of the head. The whole body becomes numb, and when all of the soul current has collected at a point between the eyebrows, breathing stops and all bodily functions cease. At that moment, the soul leaves the body and the person dies.

After a person dies, he may be required to re-enter earthly life to settle a portion of his karmic dues. If he lived his earthly life in a very degrading manner, he may have to come back to this plane under more trying circumstances. If he lived his life in an exemplary manner, he may still have to return to this lower plane to enjoy the fruits of his actions. Alternatively, depending on his actions, attachments and spiritual development, he could go to another region, whether good or bad, and remain there for a fixed time according to his karmic dues.

These are the possibilities that await the soul after a person dies. All souls receive in the next life exactly what they have earned, and they must face the consequences of their actions. If they have filled their minds with negative impressions, then these must be eradicated in some way. Once this has been done, they are free to work their way to higher planes and better conditions.*

Some people find it incredible that there is life after death and that there are other realms of existence. And yet, what could be more incredible than the fact that, as we are reading this book, our feet apparently planted firmly on the ground, we are in fact perched on the surface of a planet that is moving at a speed of 66,000 miles per hour around the sun, a ball of fire suspended in the dark universe. This is not a fairy tale but a fact. Once we understand that the way we exist in the universe is itself so incredible, should we not at least consider the possibilities that life continues after death and that there are other realms of existence?

---

* Except where otherwise mentioned, all extracts from publications integrated into the text have been drawn from Radha Soami Satsang Beas books listed at the back, for which copyright rests with RSSB. In some instances the wording has been simplified or edited for clarity in the new context.

Coming and Going

By following the teachings of the saints, we begin to release the attachments that bind us to the world. We abstain from actions whose consequences might force us to take another birth. While acknowledging that the idea of reincarnation is difficult for many people in the West to accept, Dr Johnson points out how a little reflection will prove it to be the only rational explanation of some of the most complicated questions of life. For example, why does an elderly invalid live on for years, a burden to himself and others, while a healthy child has to die suddenly?

"Only reincarnation offers any satisfactory explanation. To explain it as the inscrutable decree of a deity, arbitrarily interfering in the affairs of human life, is to invite despair and unbelief. As a matter of fact, the parents are to understand that the child, due to his own past actions, was from the very beginning allotted just that brief span of life, and they must be thankful that the child was 'loaned' to them for that brief period. The child, due to his own past actions, had been allotted just that length of life and no more. That time being finished, he had to go. His short life was only one scene, just a brief appearance, upon the stage of his career. This little act had to be played. It was also one episode in the life of the parents. When the consequences of past actions of both parents and child were paid, there was no further need for the child to remain there, no more than an actor should remain on the stage when his act is finished.

"Again, why do some people enter this life with such terrible handicaps, while others, apparently less worthy, are born in the lap of fortune? Why are some children born with superior intelligence, while others are hopelessly dull? Why are some born with criminal tendencies, while others come into life with a lively sense of purity, justice and love? These and a hundred other questions press themselves upon us all, and they have no answer, except when seen as a direct consequence of our past actions which resulted in the need to take another birth.

"Each one comes with a definite program outlined by himself, as a consequence of the actions committed by him in the past. That program he must carry out. When the last act of that program has been performed, the scene closes. The end comes. It must come. Moreover, the end cannot come until the last act of his life has been performed. He then passes to another life. There again his future is assigned to him on the basis of his own earnings. In this manner every individual marks time in the grand calendar of the ages. The only thing that can ever bring this monotonous routine to an end is the meeting with a true living spiritual teacher. When a man has this opportunity, it comes as a consequence of good actions done by him in the past, it implies that the supreme crisis of his long career has come. His deliverance is close at hand."

Some actions bring about minor repercussions, others produce more significant consequences. Sometimes the consequences of an action may be on such a large scale that they cannot be borne in one lifetime. We then have to be reborn to reap the full consequences of those actions. For example, one person intentionally throws acid in the eyes of another person and blinds him. The one who threw the acid might well have to take another birth to face the consequences of what he did. Because the action was intentionally destructive, the unavoidable result will be some sort of unfortunate experience and could even result in the person being born blind. This is strict justice, brought about as a direct result of what the person did.

One cannot escape the consequences of one's actions even if the deeds are done secretly. The consequences of all actions have to be experienced by the doer at some point in time. If we are born in certain specific conditions, it is not because of some arbitrary fate or random predeterminism. It is the direct result of what we have done in the past. In the same way, whatever we are to become in the future will be the direct result of what we do now.

Numerous books have been written on life after death and the subject of reincarnation. Many people are familiar with the studies of doctors and psychiatrists who have conducted research on people who have clinically died and then come back and told of their experiences. Some psychiatrists who have experimented with hypnosis find that when the patients are asked to go back to the time when they were in the womb, they occasionally regress even further, going back to a past life. There are numerous accounts of people all over the world who remember former lives or who possess particular virtues or skills at a very young age that normally would take a lifetime to learn. Such examples indicate a carry-over from former lives.

As suggested in the previous chapter, when a person dies, different experiences may await the soul. Being reborn on earth is only one of them. Reincarnation implies that the soul may have to return to this plane of consciousness to account for deeds done in the past.

It is not the purpose of this book to prove whether or not reincarnation or life after death exists. The reader can do his or her own research, for a lot of material on the subject is available. As with the rest of the subjects that comprise the teachings of the saints, blind faith in this area is not required. One should make a thorough inquiry into every aspect of the teachings and this subject is no different from any other. The issue of reincarnation should not bother the reader. One need not believe in reincarnation or in life after death to benefit from the teachings of the saints. In theory we may accept that there might be some truth in this way of thinking, but the only way we will ever be sure of it is by going beyond the limitations of our own physical selves and experiencing whether the statements are true or false.

Preparing for Death

We lament the death of others but rarely think constructively of our own. Actually, we would be wise to be concerned with our own end and prepare ourselves for what will then happen to us. Where will we go as we pass through death's doors? Whom are we going to meet there? Would it not be prudent to consider these questions? Religious books talk of this subject, but we rarely pay attention to them for we may believe them to be either fantasies or fairy tales, or efforts to wean people away from sin, or to persuade them to perform good deeds. The fact is that we all have to cross the gates of death. No one is an exception. Why then shut our eyes to the subject?

The time of death is clearly not the best time to begin preparing ourselves for death. It is easier to do it with time on our side, or as Lao Tzu, the Chinese mystic, says in the *Tao Te Ching*, "Manage the difficult while it is easy, manage the great while it is small. All difficult things start from the easy, all great things in the world start from the small. The journey of a thousand miles begins with a single step."

That first step, the mystics advise us, is to become aware of our attachments. It is our attachments that make us suffer and it is they, we are told, that can bring us back into this world. To paraphrase a saying from the Bible: Where your treasure is, that is where you make your home. Our treasure is whatever we care about most. If, at the time of death, we are greatly attached to people or things in the world, we will not be able to rise above these attachments. Like a magnet they will drag us back to this world: it is the mind that gives direction to our soul.

There is a lot of misunderstanding concerning attachment and detachment. Detachment does not mean renunciation. A person can renounce wealth and still be thinking about money all day, or renounce sex and be having lustful thoughts all day. Detachment means to rise above obsession and the desire to possess or own a person or thing. To become detached certainly doesn't mean that we stop loving. When a person is associated with another for some time, it is normal that a bond may develop. Attachment is the pre-occupation with someone or something to the extent that one becomes restless and loses one's balance at the thought of losing that person or that object. It includes the most common obsession—the obsession of me and mine. When we die, these attachments project themselves and fill our attention, making it very hard for us to embark on the journey beyond.

Most people would agree that it is normal practice to make preparations if one is going to travel to another country. One at least considers and makes arrangements for the means of transport and decides where one is going to stay. We are so careful in these worldly matters that we rarely undertake a big journey without making all sorts of arrangements beforehand. Yet for the one journey which everyone has to make, few people do anything. Who really considers even where that journey through death leads, or how one should prepare oneself to make it smooth?

To solve the riddle of death, philosophers through the centuries have spared no effort. But the fact is that the intellect fails. Learned and illiterate alike are helpless to find the answers. How many people must have had the same thought: How satisfying it would be if someone returned to narrate his actual experiences! We guess at what death means, but our musings are only figments of our imagination—wishful thinking to comfort us in this one dark certainty at the end of each person's life.

The saints or true spiritual teachers have solved the mystery of death. Through the work they do on themselves and the control they have of their consciousness, they can leave the human body every day and travel into other realms of existence. By learning from them we too can acquire the means to triumph over death.

They teach us that death is not to be feared. It is only the name given to the phenomenon of the soul leaving the body. Death is merely the withdrawal of the soul from the gross senses and its entrance into finer regions. It is merely giving up the present garment, namely, the body. It does not mean annihilation. There *is* life after death.

The saints have dealt with this subject at length. They have described the method of passing from one level of existence to another. By following the method of meditation prescribed by them, a disciple can learn to pass through the gates of death and return to the body at will. Only a person whose soul has travelled through the finer realms before death can understand this reality. Only experience can convey to a person what it is. Intellect is helpless to comprehend it.

This subject will be dealt with in greater detail in the chapter on meditation. For the moment we need to put it aside so that we can concentrate on the immediate issue of what one is to do first. If someone is in a house that is on fire, he will be well advised to think first of the quickest way of getting out of it before asking such questions as who set it on fire, and when and why it was set on fire. The answers to these questions can be determined after one has escaped.

Developing Our Spiritual Nature

So long as our priorities focus on the material aspects of life, we will remain frustrated and dissatisfied inside. We will achieve real balance and lasting happiness only when we rearrange our priorities taking into account our spiritual nature, and then act on those priorities. Even this first step is difficult for us because we base our priorities on our faulty perceptions of who we are.

We think we are the body. We identify ourselves with our physical form because it is the easiest part of us to see. But we need to reflect for just a moment: simply because we are in the body, does it mean we are the body? This body is changing all the time. What do we have in common with the child we were 10, 15, 25, 40 or 60 years ago? Not much. Not even a single molecule from that time is left with us. Yet we cling to the idea that this is who we are because all day long we keep our attention focused upon the sights and sounds of the physical world. The fact is that though we are in the body, we are not the body; and though we are performing certain roles in the world, we are not those roles.

If we assume that we are only physical beings, we will naturally arrange our lives, goals and priorities according to that perception. Our priorities will then mostly centre around how to acquire money, higher social standing, material security, physical beauty, better health and a host of similar external things. These priorities arise from our limited sense of who we are and limit our all-round development. All human limitations come from the one great human weakness of ego. The ego stems from the idea that we are our external personality, a physical being, the centre of every-thing. Ego is our self-centredness, our obsession with 'me, myself and I'. It is the ego that always wants to control. It is the ego that wants to possess. As long as we identify ourselves with our ego, our suffering and limitations will continue.

Mystics tell us that we are spiritual beings having a human experience, not human beings having a spiritual experience. The difference has tremendous implications and its realization helps us redefine our concept of who we are. We are spiritual beings on the path of eternity with duties to perform on the physical plane. We are not mere earthlings who will cease to exist when we die. If we realize that we are spiritual beings, then we will set our goals ac-cordingly and our priorities will automatically fall in line.

Our ego is the one barrier separating us from our spiritual na-ture. To develop spiritually we must learn to put our ego aside. This doesn't happen easily. We have to remove so many layers of greed, desire, fear, anger, selfishness and ignorance—bricks of our strong wall of ego—before we can know who we are. Ego is our major handicap. It is the bogus luggage we have accumulated on our travels, and it is by simply letting go of it that we can discover the spiritual beings we are.

A person was once admiring the sculptures of Michaelangelo and approached him in this fashion: "How can you make such exquisite sculptures?" Michaelangelo replied: "It's not difficult. I just chisel away whatever is in excess. The figures are already there." Likewise in spirituality, if we get rid of the heavy and gross layers which conceal our spiritual nature, we will become more subtle, light and free. It is not that we have to acquire any new qualities. We already have them. We just have to remove the cov-erings and let our spiritual nature come to the fore of itself.

For those who succeed in overcoming the dominance of the mind, their spiritual dimension becomes their singular reality even while living on this earth. As long as we remain engrossed in the panorama of the world, we cannot go beyond the stress and anxiety that is so characteristic of our modern life. As long as we let our senses drive us, we will keep moving away from the real treasure that exists within. As long as we continue chasing happiness in the outside world, we will continue to be frustrated. Spiritual development redirects us inwards. The expansion of consciousness will take place only when consciousness is directed inwards and upwards. The mind's habitual tendency is downwards and outwards. If we do not change its orientation, its natural inclination will continue to pull us down and into the outside world.

Saints draw attention to the spiritual and material extremes of human behaviour to help us choose where we want to go. It is for us to shape our future and to choose what we want to be. If we want to obtain a happiness and contentment that does not keep changing, saints guide us to direct our attention inwards and experience inner joy. If we want the superficial excitement which is bound to end in confusion and ultimate pain of constant change, then we can put our energies to the world around us and let ourselves be ruled by our senses. Saints call a spade a spade. They do not spare their words when describing the implications of the choices we make.

Captured by the world

On the one hand saints say there are people who roast in the fire of their desires and cravings. They are restless and dissatisfied victims of illusion, looking for happiness in what is temporary. Attachment and aversion, desire and anger, eat at their vitals and eclipse their spiritual nature. Self-gratification and repulsion keep them constantly moving back and forth between what they like and what they hate. They are driven to extremes at the goading of vanity, hatred, sex or greed. Their hearts are empty and they are constantly frustrated. Like beggars they run from one door to another and yet their hunger is never appeased. Nothing seems to awaken them to reality, not even the death of others around them. They see only the cloak, the outer covering, the body; and since the body apparently ends in a handful of dust, their lives seem to be meaningless and superficial. As far as they are concerned, their spiritual nature does not exist. The thought of developing it does not even arise, though it is the one and only thing that could make their lives better, for they have totally suppressed the most positive aspect of their nature under a multitude of heavy weights of their own making. Who, ask the saints, can possibly alleviate their secret agony, restlessness and anguish?

Enraptured by the spirit

On the other hand, saints point out that there are people who, while living in the world and carrying out their duties, remain detached. Being always aware of their spiritual nature, they remain constantly in touch with it. They live in the midst of illusion and are not deceived. They are profound and yet lead simple lives. They look down upon no one. They do not think ill of anyone nor do they deceive their fellow beings. Their thinking is crystal clear and they are efficient at whatever they do. Their hearts are open to everyone. They bear true love for all living beings. They have realized the full potential of the precious gift of the human form. They do not merely exist but live a life full of meaning, purpose and joy. They have achieved perfect balance between their worldly and spiritual duties and have escaped the stress and misery of the world. They are people who have made spirituality their number one priority, and by living the saints' teachings, they have merged their consciousness with the power behind all life.

The Boundless Infinite

The nameless was the source of heaven and earth.
It is mysterious and natural, and existed before
  heaven and earth.
Motionless and fathomless, boundless infinite;
It stands alone and never changes;
It pervades everywhere and never becomes exhausted.
It is the Mother of the Universe, from where all things
  have sprung.
I don't know its name, so I call it Tao.

From Tao Te Ching, Chapters i and xxv

Different mystics have referred to the boundless infinite as the Tao, the Shabd, the Word. Scientists call it 'creative energy' or 'vibrating energy'. Scientists, like mystics, tell us that this vibrating energy is everywhere and in every particle of the physical universe. It was this same energy that provided the force to create the universe, the force of the Big Bang that science puts at the beginning of the creation. Guru Amar Das, the third great spiritual Master of the Sikhs, says:

Through the Shabd all creation emanates,
By the Shabd it is dissolved
And through the Shabd it is created again.

Adi Granth, M.3, p. 117

26

Spiritual science and material science are in complete agreement that the creation and maintenance of our universe is brought about by a force or an all-pervading, vibrating energy. Christ says:

In the beginning was the Word, and the Word was with God, and the Word was God. The same was in the beginning with God. All things were made by him; and without him was not any thing made that was made.

John 1:1–3

It is no coincidence that Christ calls this vibrating energy the Word. As with any word, this Word is an energy that has a frequency of vibration and emits a sound. However, unlike an ordinary word, the Word has an inherent magnetic power. The Word of God to which Christ refers is not a group of symbols that can be spoken in any language, for how could that sort of word have the power to create the universe? Nor is it the written word of any scripture—be it the Bible or any other holy book. This Word refers to the infinite power behind all powers, the very life and love of the Supreme Being, a power which flows forth continuously from him. It is the very life force of the creation and it is present in everything.

Joseph Leeming, in his book *Yoga and the Bible*, explains, "It is this Word that the teachings of the saints have referred to throughout all the centuries of recorded history. Many millennia ago, it was taught by the King-Adepts and Priest-Initiates who gave initiation into the Mysteries of ancient Egypt. Later, in ancient Greece, it was given out to qualified aspirants by the Hierophants, or revealers of sacred knowledge, who presided over the Orphic and Eleusinian Mysteries. It was mentioned in the Vedas, the sacred scriptures of India. In ancient Persia, the power and practice of the divine Inner Sound was taught by Zarathustra. The Word, called the Logos in Greek, was known to the greatest of the ancient Greek philosophers such as Pythagoras, Heraclitus, Socrates and Plato. Socrates referred to hearing a mysterious Inner Sound which transported him in ecstasy to higher worlds. In ancient China, it was known as the Tao and was taught by the philosopher Lao Tzu."

Jesus taught his disciples the meaning of the Word and initiated them into its practice. For very good explanations of the teachings of Jesus on the Word, the interested reader may refer to Maharaj Charan Singh's *Light on Saint Matthew* and *Light on Saint John* and to John Davidson's *The Gospel of Jesus: In Search of His Original Teachings*. As these writings indicate, the power of the Word was known to the earliest fathers of the Christian Church, to the Essenes and Gnostics, and to the famous Egyptian philosopher Plotinus and the other Neoplatonist mystic philosophers of second- and third-century Alexandria. This power is also mentioned in the Holy Qur'an of the Muslims. Following the days of Muhammad, many renowned Muslim holy men, known as Sufis, initiated their disciples into the meaning and mysteries of the Word—the mystic Rumi being one of them.

Evidently, the teaching of the Word is not a new thing. The great mystics say that in fact it has existed since the beginning, and, under scores of different names, has been made known throughout the ages to those prepared to receive it. In his book, *God's Whisper, Creation's Thunder: Echoes of Ultimate Reality in the New Physics*, Brian Hines tells us: "Anyone who wishes to make the journey to final truth must ride upon the wave of Spirit which appears as audible vibration—the sound of Ultimate Reality. This Sound is heard not by the physical ears, but by a faculty of the soul. The mystic, Maharaj Sawan Singh, says that it 'is heard with the ears of the soul....The Sound is in reality God-in-Action....He projects Himself into everything and revels in this play....It is the unstruck music that resounds within....What we hear within is its reverberation, by gaining which the mind becomes still.' Through concentration, the energy of our consciousness is raised to a level where it can be attracted by the power of Spirit [the Word]. The soul then takes great pleasure in hearing what has been called Divine Music, or the *music of the spheres.*"*

The inner sound

Hines continues with the following observations: "The audible vibrations of Spirit have been described by spiritual scientists from many different religions, countries and times. How could it be otherwise? The essence of the Ultimate Reality will be perceived by anyone who knows how to contact it. Mystics do, of course, differ in how they describe the music of Spirit for this is conditioned by their culture and circumstances. Richard Rolle described his experience of the Holy Spirit in this fashion:

> This peace experienced by the Spirit is very sweet. A divine and dulcet melody comes down to fill it with joy. The mind is ravished with this sublime and effortless music and it sings the joy of everlasting love.... [I felt] an infusion and apprehension of heavenly spiritual sound which belonged to the song of eternal praise and to the sweetness of a melody inaccessible to normal hearing. These sounds cannot be known or heard by anybody but the one who receives them and he has to keep himself pure and separate from the world....Nobody who is absorbed in worldly matters knows anything about it....

"Here are the words of the twentieth-century Sufi mystic— Hazrat Inayat Khan—who lived almost 600 years later and half a

---

* Brian Hines, *God's Whisper, Creation's Thunder,* p. 291. The citations from Hines that follow are taken from the chapter "Principle 7: Spirit appears as audible spiritual vibration."

world away from the English mystic, Rolle. Their essential message is, however, the same:

> Abstract sound is called *saut-e sarmad* by the Sufis; all space is filled with it....The knower of the mystery of sound knows the mystery of the whole universe ...the sound of the abstract is always going on within, around, and about man. As a rule, one does not hear it because one's consciousness is entirely centred in material existence....Those who are able to hear the *saut-e sarmad* and meditate on it are relieved from all worries, anxieties, sorrows, fears and diseases; and the soul is freed from captivity in the senses and in the physical body. The soul of the listener becomes the all-pervading consciousness.

"The Chinese Taoists taught that Tao, or Spirit, could be perceived as sound. Livia Kohn says that 'in the cosmology of Taoist mystical philosophy, one may imagine the Tao as a tone of a certain wavelength that pervades and encompasses all there is. Or as the Taoist themselves have it, a certain quality of *qi* (cosmic energy) that underlies and furnishes all existence.'

"Plotinus, a mystic who came from Egypt and taught philosophy in Rome during the third century, wrote that 'energy runs through the Universe and there is no extremity at which it dwindles out.' Peter Gorman notes that 'Plotinus often speaks of the cosmos as a harmony, but the real abode of the music of the gods is the intelligible world beyond the three- dimensional cosmos. In describing the mystical journey to that world, Plotinus bids the initiate wait until he hears musical sounds proceeding from the intelligible':

> If, for instance, someone were waiting to hear a desired sound, he would withdraw from other sounds and rouse his

ear for the time when that paragon among auditory sensations should approach; so too on earth he should forego listening to perceptible sounds, unless it is strictly necessary, and preserve the psychic faculty of apprehension pure and prepare to hear tones from on high.

Plotinus

"Many more examples could be given of how conscious communion with the Word of God, or Spirit, is the common denominator of every deep religion and mystical discipline. The experiment of contemplative meditation has been replicated many times, over many centuries, in many cultures, and the results reported by serious investigators of the truth are always the same. The all-pervading conscious energy of Spirit, Tao, Saut-e-Sarmad, Holy Ghost—the name is unimportant—is perceived as audible spiritual vibration."

The inner light

"And yes, as divine light, God's light is not separate from His sound. Maharaj Sawan Singh says that 'the Word gives out both, light and sound. At this end, in the physical plane, the light and sound are lost in gross matter. On the finer planes, sound is audible and light is visible. At the upper end the Sound is the finest music, unheard by human ears—and the Light is of millions of suns and moons in one ray.' Even though the power of Spirit combines both light and sound, often perfect mystics emphasize the audible manifestation of God-in-Action. The Book of Genesis (1:3) tells us: 'And God said, Let there be light: and there was light.' This implies that the saying, the voice of God, preceded His light. Sound also tends to be the first attribute of Spirit perceived by the beginning student of contemplative meditation.

"Still, both sound and light accompany the spiritual scientist on his journey through higher domains of consciousness to the reality of God. The sound, according to perfect mystics, comes from the light, and the light comes from the sound. Electromagnetism behaves similarly: As [the scientists] Hazen and Trefil put it, 'Electricity and magnetism are two inseparable aspects of one phenomenon: you cannot have one without the other.' In the same fashion, Spirit appears in two guises to guide the soul Homeward. Maharaj Charan Singh writes, 'The Word combines both light and sound. The sound is meant to determine the direction from which it comes, and the light to enable us to travel towards it.'

"...Maharaj Seth Shiv Dayal Singh explains that there are five spiritual sounds corresponding to the five regions of creation: 'Each region has its own distinctive Sound and its own characteristic secret....It is via the Sound of each region that the soul can, by degrees, ascend from one region to another, up to the highest stage.'"

The question then is why can't we hear or see the Word, the Spirit? Hines says in an earlier passage: "Physicist Nick Herbert notes that 'there is a close parallel between the senses of vision and hearing because both involve sensing the frequencies of certain vibrations.' He says that physical vision is 'a subjective appreciation of electromagnetic vibrations possessing wavelengths between 400 and 700 nanometers [billionths of a meter], otherwise known as 'light'...the ear is sensitive to sound frequencies between 20 cycles and 20,000 cycles per second.' The human body is incapable of sensing vibrations outside of these ranges.

"Spirit is a non-material vibration of God-in-Action, and so cannot be seen or heard by the physical eyes or ears—no matter how sensitive those organs might be. Indeed, perceptions of material phenomena pull our consciousness outward and downward, away from the point where Spirit can be contacted. We are not aware of this soul-power because our attention is diffused, rather than concentrated. Just as the energy within a tank of gasoline would be equivalent to the superforce if it could be focused upon a single proton, so it is possible for our consciousness to become one with Spirit if it could be withdrawn to a single point. As Jesus said, 'If therefore thine eye be single, thy whole body shall be full of light' (Matt. 6:22). And sound.

"Maharaj Sawan Singh writes that 'the Word is ringing in every atom. We do not hear it because we are not in touch with it within ourselves.' What prevents us from contacting this immanent power? Lack of concentration. Perfect knowledge, bliss, and love are within us, not without. Yet virtually all our attention is scattered outside, in material sensations, thoughts, images, imagination and emotions. Inner realms remain unknown, *terra incognita*. Even if we manage to close our eyes and forget the outside world for a moment, awareness of our physical body remains. This too keeps us bound to limited reality.

"Maharaj Charan Singh writes, 'Spirit is even now in our body. The soul is only a ray of that Spirit and the soul is spread in the whole body ...we have to withdraw that consciousness back to the eye centre to be attracted to that Spirit, then it will pull the soul upwards. Spirit is everywhere, but you have to withdraw your consciousness to that stage where the Spirit can pull the soul like a magnet.'

"...Contemplative meditation elevates the soul to a plane of consciousness where it unites with the all-pervading conscious energy of Spirit. This bears some resemblance to the launch of a space shuttle. Consider *soul* to be the command vehicle which is to be lifted into space. *Mind* is the powerful rocket on top of which that vehicle sits. Our *body* is the launching pad and gantries that support the various components of the space shuttle. The mission, the *over-arching goal*, is to place the command vehicle—soul—in a high 'orbit.'

"The launching pad of our body plays an important role in preparing for this mission. Our physical senses, after all, are the means by which we learn about meditation and the other research methods of spiritual science. But just as the gantries which supply the space shuttle drop away in the final seconds before lift-off, so must we become detached from materiality—including our body—before mystical transport into higher domains of consciousness occurs. The power for this transport initially comes from mind, which serves as the engine for overcoming the pull of the physical senses and thoughts about this world.

"...In contemplative meditation the spiritual scientist repeats words associated with non-material planes of existence. This gradually pulls the mind away from the lowest domain of creation, just as the engines of the shuttle's booster rockets cause it to rise above the launch pad—barely moving at first, then more and more rapidly until it disappears into the clouds. The command vehicle of the soul is controlling the engine of the mind, but cannot rise up without its power....

"However, after reaching a certain height those rockets drop away, and the command vehicle travels on under its own power. Similarly, [at a certain level] the soul leaves the mind...and the Spirit becomes the motive force for mystical transport. This force is audible as sound, and visible as light. It is the divine dynamo which energizes every part of creation. Maharaj Charan Singh says, '...this Sound not only leads us but actually takes us back to the Father. First we follow it; then as we make internal progress, we merge into it and ride, or ascend, to our home by means of the Sound, the Word. It is constantly pulling us inside like a magnet and attracting us homeward.' "

The Five Pillars of a Spiritual Life

Saints have a very positive and optimistic view of us. Though they may note our predicament, our current situation, what they really see is what we can become. They know that each person can become a perfect being, full of light and joy. They also know that most of us are unaware of this fact because our minds have been clouded by worldly attachments and scattered by wrong activities to such an extent that we have lost sight of where we can find real peace and joy.

Once we understand our great potential, we will naturally apply ourselves to developing what is lying dormant within us. We will make sure that we take positive actions that nourish spiritual growth, and avoid negative or destructive actions that stunt it.

To help us avoid the many pitfalls that lie between us and our goal, the saints advise us to concentrate our efforts on five main points:

1. To follow the instructions of a true living teacher
2. To abstain from eating meat, fowl, fish and eggs
3. To lead an honest, moral life
4. To refrain from taking drugs and alcohol
5. To practise meditation for two and a half hours a day

These are the five pillars that will support and sustain our spiritual nature. These are the practices which will protect and develop our self. Without them, we would find it difficult to realize if we were going astray. Like the railroad tracks or the painted lines on a highway, they help us keep on spiritual track and stay on the right road. They give direction to our life. When we step outside these practices, we can be sure that we are going away from our goal. These five principles provide an excellent and practical guide to safeguard, strengthen and increase our spiritual development.

The Need for a Living Spiritual Teacher

Ever since there have been human beings on this earth, there have also been spiritual teachers, saints or mystics to show us the real purpose of life. As explained earlier, the terms saint, mystic and spiritual teacher as used throughout this book apply to a person who has conquered his or her mind, elevated his consciousness to the highest spiritual regions, seen the reality of God face to face and merged with that reality.

The first and most fundamental principle of the saints' teachings is that in order for us to achieve God-realization, we need the guidance of a living teacher. For something as simple as learning how to drive, we need a teacher. If we want to learn to fly an airplane, we cannot do it by just reading manuals and books. If, while we are learning to fly, we don't have a teacher with us, we will crash. How much more, then, will a living teacher be needed to learn how to cross the dense reality of daily life safely, to face the complexity of the world without losing our balance, to learn how to enter the more subtle planes of existence and to travel through them—those fine inner regions which the soul has to pass through once it leaves the physical plane.

Spirituality is a highly involved and complex subject. For travelling through the inner regions, it is necessary to have a guide who knows those regions and travels through them himself. Until we are in contact with a person who is thoroughly conversant with every detail of the inner regions so that we can benefit from his experience, we will find it very difficult to move in this direction at all.

No person in this world—no matter how intelligent, loving or religious—can help us go into these inner regions unless he himself has passed through them. Just as we need a guide to lead us when we travel through unfamiliar and dangerous terrain in the outer world, so we need a guide on the inner planes. Unless someone has already reached and crossed these subtle planes, how could we be confident that he or she could even meet us on the other side of death? Similarly, unless a person has himself experienced God-realization, how can he take us back to the Lord?

We actually stand in need of a teacher the moment we are born. Whether it is at home, at school or in life, we learn best from others. There is hardly a skill or profession in the world that can be mastered without a teacher. How then can we conceive of learning, without a teacher, this most difficult subject of spiritual science? Its requirements are far more exacting and the need for a teacher far more urgent than any other subject we can imagine. Not only must our teacher guide us throughout our life, but he or she must also be with us and guide us beyond death.

Once we accept that we will always learn best from another human being and that spirituality is not a matter of blind faith but a science like any other, we start to accept and appreciate the need for a spiritual teacher. The great mystics or saints come to earth for this very work. They come, not to make the physical world a better place, but to reveal to us the way of spiritual realization so as to free us from the endless bondage of birth and death. The following parable may illustrate this point:

Imagine for a moment that there are many people incarcerated in a jail. A humanitarian comes along and, seeing that the inmates do not get cool drinking water during the summer months, arranges for ice to be sent to them daily. Another arrives, and seeing that they get coarse and unpalatable food, he arranges for delicious dishes to be regularly distributed to them. A third one, also taking pity on the prisoners, provides them with warm blankets during the cold weather. All three humanitarians have doubtless succeeded in lessening to some extent the hardships of prison life, but the people still remain imprisoned. They are still in jail! High walls still separate them from the world outside and the hope for freedom still remains an empty dream.

Then another person appears on the scene. He has the key to the prison gate. He opens the gate and liberates the prisoners so that they are free to go back to their homes. There can be no doubt that the deed of the last person addresses the real need of the prisoners in a way that the charitable deeds of the previous three do not.

Mystics often depict this world as a vast prison house. There is only one exit from this prison—the human life—and its secret is known to the saints alone. A saint, therefore, is the one who has the key and can open the door. Only a saint can guide us along the hidden escape route that is the inner spiritual path and remove us from our suffering in a way that no one else can.

The saints of the past were doubtless true spiritual teachers, but we cannot benefit from them now. We need a living teacher of the present day. Just as a sick man has to consult a doctor who is living and cannot take treatment from a doctor of the past—no matter how famous the doctor was—so too we need a living spiritual teacher. Only a living spiritual teacher can help us unravel the complexity of life that entangles us from day to day.

A living teacher is essential to reveal to us the inner reality of the spirit. If we could do without a living teacher for God-realization, then past saints need never have come to earth in the human form. If the saints of the past could help us today without being present among us, then what need was there for them to come to earth at all? If God, without the intermediary of a living human embodiment of his qualities, could today draw souls to that same high spiritual state, then where would be the need for a spiritual teacher to be present in the world? In short, if there was the need for spiritual teachers to come in the human form at certain points in history, then surely there is an equal need today. The fact is that a living teacher is an absolute necessity for the spiritual path. Christ too, in his own time, said: "As long as I am in the world, I am the light of the world" (John 9:5). Saints and mystics of all countries and times have stressed the need for a living guide on the inner journey.

The way of the spiritual teacher

Our concept of the higher realms remains no more than a mental concept until we have experienced them ourselves. It is no more than a projection of our mind, a figment of our imagination. A true spiritual teacher or saint, however, does not function from mental concepts, projections of the mind or from what he has read in books. A true spiritual teacher speaks from his own experience. Since the mystics have merged into the highest state of bliss and union with God, they explain what they have experienced.

True mystics never advocate that we should change our religion. They come to unite, not to divide. The sun has many rays, and when we look at them, they may seem different from each other, but when we look up at their source we see that they are all in essence one and the same. We may refer to God as Jehovah, Jesus, Allah, Krishna, cosmic energy or by any other name, but what we all want in reality is to get in contact with that same Truth. True spirituality has nothing to do with the rites and rituals of our religions; its main concern is to explore the love that is to be found in all of us, regardless of how we express it. Inside us there are no boundaries. We want to rediscover our own natural heritage—that treasure that lies inside us—and how to do this is precisely what the true spiritual teachers come to teach. They themselves have merged back into their source, their primal home. To do this, they leave their body at will, travel to the highest spiritual regions and come back at will to continue to instruct their disciples so that they too may learn to do the same.

True spiritual teachers don't come to change the world. They make it clear through their teachings that this world is not meant to be a paradise. If they so intended, the great saints and mystics of the past would have made it a paradise by now.

Instead, saints intend to teach us how to collect our consciousness and merge it with the sweet melody of God's spirit. Once in contact with the inner music, the mind travels with it to its very source, and finds its lost home. The soul, which was paralysed in the wilderness of the mind, discovers its separate identity, and triumphant, it too reunites with its source.

Signs of a true spiritual teacher

A true spiritual teacher never charges anything nor does he accept donations for his teachings. The saints' teachings are free, like all the other bounties of nature such as air, water and sunlight. A true spiritual teacher is never a beggar nor a burden to anyone, and always supports himself and his family by earning his own livelihood. In this day and age it is very difficult to find a true spiritual teacher who is solely interested in helping people and not interested in their money. A true spiritual teacher is never opposed to those who do not share his convictions, nor does he complain about the conduct of others. He does not criticize or slander others. A true spiritual teacher is humble and discreet, and keeps his powers hidden. He does not perform miracles like a magician to please his audience. His main goal is to instruct his disciples on how to meditate on the Word or the Shabd to achieve God-realization, and how to live their daily life so as to strengthen this spiritual work.

Advantages of having a living spiritual teacher

A saint alone knows everything about death. At the time of death, when family, wealth, possessions and body all leave us, it is the true spiritual teacher alone who stays with the disciple. He, the perfect master-teacher, is with us as we pass through death's door. After death, it is he who acts as our guide in the spiritual regions.

The further we progress in our study of mysticism, the more obvious it becomes that we cannot do without a living teacher. Our teacher, friend, guide, the living example of our ideal, becomes the central pillar and support for our spiritual growth.

We derive endless advantages when we receive directions and advice from a living master. He enables us to be better persons—more loving, more efficient, more caring—and to better fulfil our responsibilities from day to day. He helps us raise our consciousness above the reach of mind and matter. By following his instructions we are metamorphosed as we contact God's power within us. It is the magic of this power that breaks us free from all our limitations.

Just as a jeweller can take a rough diamond and, by removing whatever is in excess, can transform it into a precious gem, similarly, the spiritual teacher makes the disciple aware of his or her own dross as well as his or her own inherent spirituality. When we come in contact with a true, living spiritual teacher we discover our precious essence and we learn how to develop and bring forth this essence to the fullest.

Why Vegetarianism?

Each year thousands of acres of rainforests are burnt to prepare them for cattle farming. Big, strong and beautiful trees are chopped down in order to plant pastures to raise livestock. This is done on such a large scale that it is already affecting the weather of the world. Moreover, in areas where water is scarce, the meat industry takes away thousands of gallons of water daily to raise cattle and fowl. Similarly, to meet the market demand, the fish industry is dramatically affecting the ecosystem of the oceans. Each year thousands of dolphins die in the nets that are used to trap tuna. An unknown number of aquatic species have already become extinct while others are on the verge of extinction. Ecologically and socially the price we pay is very high. It is morally wrong, unnecessary from a health point of view, and much more expensive to feed ourselves on cattle, fish, fowl and their eggs. We could meet our needs for protein from foods of vegetable origin more simply and economically, and not have to tax so heavily the animals, the forests, ourselves and the planet.

The toxins and disease organisms in the flesh of animals transmit illness to humans. The concentration of uric acid in animal food places a burden upon the human body that is very hard to eliminate and is the cause of all types of health-related problems. If we study our bodies closely, we will see that we were not genetically engineered to eat meat. Our teeth and nails are not like those of carnivorous animals, and our intestines are long—unlike those

43

of meat-eating animals—which makes our capacity to eliminate animal toxins dangerously slow.

Ponder over the fate of millions of cows, goats, fish, sheep and chickens that are butchered every year for us to cook and eat! We kill them without so much as a thought—mercilessly—or at best we have others butcher them on our behalf. How unmindful and unconcerned we remain about their suffering! Do we ever face these facts? It is senseless that all this pain is inflicted, and these economic, ecological and social problems are caused, to give pleasure to our taste buds for a few short minutes. What we do not realize is that when we base our happiness on the suffering of other beings, we bring upon ourselves negative and undesirable consequences.

One can be a vegetarian for health, social, humane, economic, ethical or ecological reasons. However, the reason saints advise us to abstain completely from taking meat of any kind is spiritual. It is based on the law of karma or compensation which can be summed up in the Biblical saying: "As ye sow, so shall ye reap" (Gal. 6:7). The burden we carry of destructive actions we have done in the past is already heavy and weighs us down; we should stop adding to this load we have unknowingly put upon ourselves. If we sow suffering, one day we have to reap suffering. If we kill for our food or pay others who have killed on our behalf, we are responsible for every iota of suffering we cause. We are inviting pain on ourselves in amounts equivalent to the pain we inflict. Even if it means we have to come back to the creation in another life, we have to meet the consequences of our actions one day. This law of equivalent compensation, just as Newton's law in physics, is precise, unavoidable and unchanging.

It is very difficult to leave this plane of consciousness if we are responsible, directly or indirectly, for the killing of animals. The debt is just too big and will have to be paid. It is for this reason that true spiritual teachers advise us to stop feeding ourselves with the blood and pain of other beings. They want us to stop adding weight to our already heavy load of karmas.

A needle is naturally attracted towards a magnet, but if we put a heavy weight on the needle it cannot be pulled to the magnet. In the same way, if we keep putting heavy weights on ourselves that keep us at the lower levels of creation, it will be impossible for us to make spiritual progress.

Leading a Simple, Moral Life

The way we conduct our lives has direct impact on the development of our spiritual nature. All spiritual teachers tell us that sound moral conduct is the very foundation of a spiritual life.

The saints' teachings on ethics are based on their knowledge of which actions are beneficial and which are harmful for spiritual development. Saints are not concerned with morality only for the sake of morality. Their concern is to help us understand the law of action and reaction that governs the world. They want to lead us away from traps and illusions. They know that in our obsession with pleasure we look for happiness in places where we can only become frustrated, unhappy and attached. The moral guidelines the saints give are to prevent us from falling into the dangerous cycle of actions and reactions that binds us to the creation.

The question of sex

The mystics advise people to regulate sexuality because it pulls the attention downwards into the body. If we are to grow in spirituality, our aim should be to raise our attention upwards—to raise our level of consciousness. Anything which draws the attention into the sensual pleasures of the body pulls one down into the world and so serves to keep one more tightly bound to the physical creation.

Stanley White, discussing in his book *Liberation of the Soul* the moral issues that confront a disciple on the spiritual path, points out that many spiritual teachers are themselves married.

He says: "They show us that one can lead the life of a householder yet still practice the mystic path successfully. If we live a sensible, controlled life, we will find that our meditation will slowly detach us from physical needs. Then we will not miss the 'loss' of sex, for the mind will have found a superior pleasure (within) and will gladly give up the pleasures associated with sex. Mystics are very practical; they know that we cannot stop indulging in the sensual pleasures the moment we come to the path. They teach that it is a gradual and slow withdrawal. Therefore, they allow us to conservatively satisfy bodily needs until we reach the state where the need is overcome through attachment to the spirit within.

"Practically, then, our interest in and need for sex decreases as we make spiritual progress within. A life of celibacy would be impractical for all but a mere handful who have, in fact, transcended this need. Similarly, a forced celibacy would accomplish nothing since the mind would be constantly rebelling, due to repression. So, it is obvious that the prescription given by the saints, namely, living a clean, moral life within the confines of marriage, with an aim toward slow and gradual detachment—by attaching oneself to the power within—is the only logical method whereby the bodily needs can be transcended."

It is the mind that keeps us from experiencing the spirit. Therefore, most people who want to develop their spiritual understanding try in one way or another to subdue the mind. Some practise various forms of penances or live lives of great austerity. By so doing they hope to detach the mind forcibly from the pleasures of the world. But if we do not give the mind an alternative source of pleasure, if we fail to attach it to some more enjoyable source of bliss, then one day the mind will react. The monk who returns to the world after achieving strict self-discipline may find himself overwhelmed when faced with the temptations of the world. He may lose even the normal self-control that an ordinary man possesses. When the mind is simply bound and tied and forced into submission, then, when freed, it often returns to the pleasures of the body with redoubled strength.

Detachment from sensual pleasures cannot be achieved by repression. Nor, contrary to what some people may think, can we rise above the sensual pleasures by indulging in them. This is like trying to stop a fire by throwing gasoline on it. The mind will only become more active. It will never become satiated through indulging it. Rather, indulgence will increase its desires. Saints suggest a different approach. They advise us to attach the mind to something higher, something that will give much more pleasure than the sensual pleasures—and this higher pleasure is our contact with the Word. The Word is the primordial source of pure and everlasting pleasure. The divine rapture produced by contact with that ceaseless Melody keeps one so entranced within oneself that one never tires of it. In comparison to it, one will find the worldly pleasures insipid and of no interest. Only in this way can one be really detached.

Detachment can never be achieved in a vacuum. Only attachment to something better—to the Word—can produce true detachment from the world.

Less is more

Saints advise us to be honest in our dealings with others and to make our moral code inseparable from our life. They put great importance on the necessity of everyone earning his or her own living, for if we live from the earnings of others, we create another obstacle to our own progress and growth. By being a burden on others we create debts that extend the time we have to spend at this plane of consciousness so they can be repaid.

True spiritual teachers stand before us as examples of honest living. They support themselves without losing their way in the process. They never accept money from their disciples for their own personal use. Their dealings with everyone are sincere and straightforward. They demonstrate from moment to moment that happiness does not lie in wealth and possessions but in contentment of the heart.

In this materialistic age we have somehow bought the idea that we need more of everything to be happy. Little do we realize that when material comforts and security become the most important thing for us, our inner life begins to wither away. By attaching ourselves to money, possessions and things of the world, we strengthen our egos, weaken our inner focus or balance, and, in the process, alienate ourselves from who we are. This is how we lose our peace of mind, and, possessed by our possessions and our ambitions, become anxious and stressed.

Trying always to ignore the stark reality of our own impermanence, our mind deludes itself by keeping busy, trying to amass more wealth, more power or whatever it most enjoys. In this scenario we can all too easily become workaholics, with little time to remember our final end. In reality we are doing little more than the ostrich that hides its head in the ground and thinks no one can see it. Our end has to come one day, no matter where we hide or what we are busy doing.

In our attempts to find happiness in things outside of ourselves, we have increased the complexity of our lives to a point of no return. We have allowed the marketing media to brainwash us, creating artificial necessities. In the process, we have moulded ourselves after the promised heavens of TV commercials and fallen headlong into their enticing traps.

Mass marketing media, the face of human greed, has replaced our spiritual values with material ideals. Consumerism dictates the way we live. Going shopping has become a substitute for religious experience and the malls and shopping complexes have become the new places of worship. We need to keep up with the Joneses and what the media projects to us. Ten credit cards are hardly sufficient. Even if we own a house for winter, another for summer, an apartment on the ocean and a cabin in the woods, we are still not content.

How many shirts can we wear in a day? How many dresses can we parade in an evening? In how many rooms can we sleep at night? Even if we succeed in obtaining material things that represent the ultimate in status—a customized Rolls, maybe, or a private jet, what will we do if we find that we're still not happy? Will we be like the dog madly chasing a car till it catches up with it, but then finds that it doesn't know what to do?

Greed is destructive. Greed blinds a person. It makes people so obsessed with getting their perceived share of the proverbial cake that they are ready to sell their souls for a song. In their short-sighted demands for satisfaction, without realizing it, people often become ruthless. Just consider how we have raped the earth's resources to satisfy our greed. When convenient, we compromise with principles that we say are important to us. When it suits us, we find justifications for the very actions that we condemn in others.

Greed and the relentless pursuit of self-gratification harden a person's heart, scatter the mind and waste precious energy, making spiritual development very difficult to achieve.

Rich is the person who has not the most, but who is happy with whatever he or she has. We have raised our standard of living, and sadly lost our sense of contentment. Contentment has become almost a foreign word in today's vocabulary and yet we have so much more than we really need.

If we take the trouble to think about it, we will realize we don't need that much. Our necessities are not that many. Life is very simple. It is we who complicate it. The more we possess, the more we are possessed. The less we possess, the less we are possessed.

Maharaj Charan Singh in one of his discourses quoted in *Treasure Beyond Measure* tells us: "Ask anybody and you will find that he has no time. The labourer has no time; the engineer has no time; the doctor has no time; the industrialist has no time. Who has time to relax? Who has some moments of leisure? No one.

"What then have we gained from all this progress, from all these developments? We cannot find an hour for ourselves, not even half an hour in which to relax. Everybody is suffering from mental tension—every face reflects tension—no one appears to be relaxed. Four people cannot sit together and shake off their tension in laughter and relaxation.

"The result is increasing incidence of heart disease, diabetes and high blood pressure. Our entire life has become artificial. We have forgotten how to laugh, and how to shed tears. Our smiles have become artificial, our tears have become artificial.

"This is not entirely the fault of development. We have become prisoners of the things that development and progress have given us. These things were meant for our benefit, for our use; we were not meant for their benefit, for their use. But we have become slaves of the machinery, not its owners. We are possessed by it; we do not possess it. We should become the owners, the masters of all this progress. Every person should get enough food, should have shelter over his head, should be relaxed, should be free from tension. There should be no tension on anyone's mind.

"Parents should be loving towards their children, and children should have respect for their parents. These are the values which every human being cherishes in life. These are the basic values of life. If the values of life are lost, then what is the advantage of all this development? What is the benefit of all this progress?

"I am not against modern developments and the present civilization. But at no cost should we compromise with the basic values of human life. There should be leisure for us. We should lead a simple, relaxed and tension-free life. There should be unity and peace in the family, respect for our elders, and we should look after our children. Our food and environment should be healthy.

We should be sympathetic and helpful to others. Our developments should lead us in this direction."

If we build our world on the false promises presented to us by the media, we will be swept away by the media's shallowness and artificiality—all driven by nothing but greed. By throwing away this opportunity to develop ourselves fully, we will also lose our chance to achieve lasting peace of mind and the incomparable happiness and joy that lies within.

Clouding our Vision

Drugs: false doors of perception

The aim of spiritual life is to achieve freedom from illusion. If we take mind-altering substances, whether chemical or natural, we may well experience other realities or different states of awareness, but none of them last and they are all limited to the realm of the mind. It would be very simple if we could take a pill and increase our awareness permanently, but unfortunately that is not the case. With drugs, the moment the effect is gone, one becomes again the same person one was before. Experiences with drugs are just mental states and have nothing to do with spiritual experience, and that is why the experiences of people who take drugs differ from each other.

Spiritual experiences on the other hand do not differ from each other. All spiritual experience is bound to be the same as it arises from an inner journey whose landmarks are there to be seen by all. It is not a figment of the individual imagination.

Drugs may give one a little physical concentration and may put one in a semi-trance or seemingly blissful state, but when the trip is over, so is the experience. Even if one sees something in an altered state of awareness, one has no control over it, whereas spiritual experience is something over which we have control. Through spiritual practice we can change our level of consciousness and travel the spiritual realms when we want to, and in the same way we can come back to the body level of consciousness whenever we want to.

Spiritual experience develops our awareness of the soul and makes us much finer and better people. We are no longer victims of our senses; we control our mind, and the mind starts controlling the senses. But by taking drugs, we remain slaves of both mind and senses. By creating more illusions we will not help ourselves wake up from the illusion we are already in.

Alcohol: deadly message in a bottle

The necessity of abstaining from alcoholic drinks does not need much logic to support it. We all know what fools we make of ourselves when drunk, and what follies and crimes are committed under the influence of alcohol. Its use so clouds our vision and distorts our sense of values that our sense of discrimination fails us and we are unable to see what actions will do harm to us or others. Even moderate amounts of alcohol can prevent clear thinking. The basic aim of a seeker for truth is to become more conscious, not less.

Concentration is an essential part of meditation. Concentration demands that we be alert and present to ourselves. If we are under the influence of drugs or alcohol we might feel good for a while and drift into an ocean of oblivion, but serious spiritual practice is impossible under the influence of alcohol or drugs.

Meditation

Real spiritual growth can be achieved only through the practice of meditation. There are many ways to meditate, and each method varies in its results and purposes. The meditation described here is the technique of uniting the soul with the primordial power or Shabd. It is simply and solely concerned with uniting us with our source.

To be able to make contact with this power that manifests within us as inner light and sound, we need to follow the technique of meditation prescribed and taught by a spiritual teacher who is himself in contact with it. If we have a radio that is disconnected from its source of energy, then obviously we would not be able to hear any music from it. To tune it to a broadcasting frequency, we would have to find a way to connect the radio to a source of power. In the same way a true, living spiritual teacher, being tuned in to the source of energy that created the universe, is able to show us how to reconnect ourselves to the inner spiritual music that is resounding within each and every one of us.

The inward journey

Life may be considered a journey. The first plane of this journey is the one we are travelling on now in which we associate ourselves with the world through the senses. Though we may experience many moments of happiness in this plane, there is also plenty of frustration and suffering. The so-called pleasures we can enjoy at this level will always be transformed into pain or disillusionment with time. Limited by our senses and worldly attachments that hold us captive, we remain confined to this world and oblivious to all else. We have no idea of the second plane of the journey—the journey inward.

Lasting happiness is attained by beginning the second plane of the journey. We ascend to this plane through meditation. It starts to happen the moment we begin to raise our consciousness through the body and concentrate it at the spiritual eye focus. This focus is the natural seat of the mind and soul in the physical body—a point about midway between, and slightly above, the two eyes. It is a subtle spiritual point and cannot be found by physically dissecting the body. It is at this subtle point that the mind and the soul are knotted together, the resting point of our consciousness in the waking state. And it is here, if we raise our consciousness to this level, that we contact the Shabd, or the enrapturing music of God.

When, through the practice of meditation, we come in contact with the bliss of the divine melody, the same mind that is constantly running after sensual pleasures becomes completely subdued. The pleasures of the world become utterly insipid. When we mould our life towards the aim of contacting the divine melody, our life will become more meaningful and worth living.

Dying while living

It is true that the treasure of the Shabd lies within us. It is our wealth. It is there for us. But we will discover it only when we practise the technique of meditation taught by a living teacher—a perfect master of the spirit.

Only a true living mystic can teach the technique of meditation by which we withdraw our consciousness from the entire body, up to the spiritual eye centre, where we come in contact with the

Sound Current. The mystics refer to this process of meditation as 'dying while living'.

As explained before, when death comes, our soul withdraws upwards from the soles of the feet and comes to the spiritual eye centre. First the feet become cold; then the legs become cold; then the whole body becomes numb and the organs of the body cease to function. When the soul goes through the spiritual eye centre, then the body, lacking the soul, cannot survive and we die.

By the same process in meditation we die while living. According to the teachings of the saints, meditation is the process by which the entire life consciousness leaves the lower body and the soul current is concentrated at the spiritual eye. We are then able to break through the physical plane and the soul's real journey homeward begins.

The essential difference between ordinary death and dying while living is that in meditation the soul's link with the body is not broken. The organs of the body continue to function, and the soul returns to the body at the end of meditation.

When the attention is functioning below the eyes, we are dead as far as the real and everlasting life is concerned. When the attention is withdrawn and concentrated at the spiritual eye centre, we become truly alive and are dead as far as the world is concerned.

Conquering death

One of the benefits of the teachings of the saints is that a disciple crosses the gates of death in a conscious state of happiness. This is the experience of the disciples who have diligently followed the instructions of a true spiritual teacher. It is not merely talk or a fable taken from scriptures. Those who strictly follow the instructions of a true spiritual teacher can reach the state of dying daily while living. Once they achieve this exalted condition, they can go into the regions above, and then come back into the same physical body at will. For them God is a living reality. They have conquered death.

To die while living is the chief motivation in spirituality because it is only after such death that the soul comes really alive. Dying while living has nothing to do with committing suicide or being cremated, or buried. Rather, if one learns this art, one can end the cycle of birth and rebirth and live forever. Being able to cross the gates of death, the disciple loses all fear of dying.

We can never realize true life until we go beyond the domain of death, or, in other words, until we are reborn into the subtle higher regions. That is why Christ says: "Except a man be born again, he cannot see the Kingdom of God" (John 3:3). If one masters this technique, one need never return to the suffering of this world again.

Instant results?

Dying while living is not accomplished easily. Only they who have subdued the mind, dissolved all desires and cravings and annihilated the ego can gain this experience. It is not as easy to obtain as it is to read or to talk about, for one can achieve it only by letting go of the world. So long as worldly desires control the body, the soul cannot leave it. It is only by detaching oneself from the body and mind that one can die while living.

Some people mistakenly believe that one can merge into God-consciousness in the twinkling of an eye. But there are no shortcuts in spirituality. Real alchemy is the process of transmuting base metals (this mortal life) into gold (immortality) and that takes time and effort. Don't be under any illusions! Achieving this condition doesn't happen overnight. It is a steady process of transformation, not of information.

When we undertake any task, we are often anxious to get quick results. Being result-oriented may work in the business world, but, in spirituality, things are different and they often seem contradictory. The first thing—if we want results—is to forget about results.

In the beginning we need to give less attention to the result, and more to effort. This attitude helps us to be more skilful in our work and to solve the problems as they emerge on our path. If we take care of the moment, automatically we take care of the future.

The attitude needed in spirituality is different from what is needed in the material world. Spirituality demands that we modify our worldview, become more humble in our approach to life—with no great expectations—just like a child learning to write. The child is absorbed in learning, practising, just doing it—with no expectations. The transformation from novice to expert takes time. It takes patience, the will to put in the effort, and the will to struggle as long as necessary.

The warrior within

Our higher mind and our downward tendencies engage in a life-long battle and the struggle continues until one side is victorious. To win this fight for our higher mind, we must rely on endurance, proper effort and the guidance and support of the living teacher. If we see the world as it is, if we are tired of running from ourselves and the anguish of loneliness, if we see that we are simply looking everywhere for substitutes for love, then we have no other option but to be bold enough to struggle.

This inner struggle will be difficult. Do we want to go through the hardships of letting our attachments go? If so, are we ready to make the sacrifices that are necessary to acquire a new way of seeing and doing things? Think about it. There are many spiritual paths. This one is not meant for everybody. It requires a lot of courage, patience and persistence.

There is an anecdote taken from the life of the famous painter Picasso that illustrates this point. Once, while visiting one of his last exhibitions, a lady approached him: "Maestro, your paintings are very beautiful," she said, "but tell me, couldn't a child paint the same way you do?" "*Si*, you are absolutely right," said Picasso, "the only difference is that it took me ninety years to paint like a child."

It took Picasso a lot of time, hard work, and patience to acquire the simplicity of a child again. Likewise, we have to work hard, but we can bring that innocence, that simplicity and that purity back to our lives. By relying on the five pillars of spirituality, our whole worldview will become different. It will become more relaxed, more loving and more fruitful.

Picasso had to unlearn everything he had learned to become child-like again. That is the approach we need in our life. When we are established in spirituality, we live in the here-and-now, and the question of result doesn't arise. We become result-oriented when we don't want to be where we are; when we want to arrive at the result without putting in the effort; when we miss the opportunity to enjoy the effort itself. Meditation is the effortless effort that brings simplicity and purity back to our lives.

Letting go of our attachments

Meditation is the medicine that will cure us from the suffering that we have brought upon ourselves. If we want this medicine to work, we have to let go of many attachments and meaningless pursuits that further complicate the illusion in which we live. Through meditation alone can we learn to let go of our attachments before we die.

Our lives should not revolve around any attachments—whether they are people, pets, objects, jobs, roles or projects. By quietening the mind, meditation helps us to think more clearly and to put things in their proper perspective. By the practice of meditation we become aware that we will be here in this world for only a certain time. Nothing belongs to us, nor do we belong to anyone. We are all just passing through. There is nothing to get hung-up on. We can let go of our attachments. We can let go of everything that doesn't last.

Meditation makes us aware that everything in life is transitory. No matter how much time we devote to something, be it our own body, another person, work or anything else, eventually, at the time of death, we will have to let it go. Whether we want to or not, we will have to let go of everything. So what the mystics are telling us is to let go, in our hearts, of all these attachments before we die; and the sooner we let go of them in our hearts, the happier we will be.

As stated before, in meditation we learn to quieten the mind. When the mind becomes settled, we begin to see that we are apart from our mind. Meditation helps us to become free from the habit of judging, which strengthens our ego, and from the thinking processes which create our illusions. When the mind becomes free from judging and when the current of thoughts settles down, we begin to see where we really stand. We might not like it. But the only way to make any progress is to accept our secret devils and to recognize our weaknesses, and then to work on them. An alcoholic, a drug addict or an obsessed person cannot begin to cure himself or herself until he or she acknowledges and accepts the basic problem. It is essential to know ourselves as we are before we can change.

The attachments and obsessions that we so ardently cling to only make us suffer. They delay our spiritual journey and make it harder for us to begin to live fully. They perpetuate the illusion that we belong here. But we don't belong here. This is not our real home. Here everything is changing and will not last. The only thing that exists here permanently is our true self, the Shabd, which is awareness eternal, existence eternal, and bliss eternal. The only way to get in contact with this eternal self, to realize what we really are, is through meditation.

Only meditation goes deep enough to uproot our problems. Wishful thinking, mental affirmations and various types of therapies just scratch at the surface. They may work for a while, but after some time their power evaporates and we go back to our habitual ways of behaviour. These methods are like taking aspirin for cancer. Meditation on the Word or Shabd strikes at the root of our problems by dissolving our attachments, and by putting us in contact with the primordial source of power and joy.

Meditation helps us develop our latent positive qualities. It dissolves the blocks that prevent them from coming to the fore. By the correct practice of meditation, we get closer to the core of our being, and then, automatically, our positive qualities begin to show themselves. They come up to the surface of our being just like cream rises naturally in milk. Through meditation our downward tendencies turn around. Anger becomes tranquillity, lust becomes indifference, greed becomes contentment, ego becomes humility, and attachment becomes real love.

As we become aware of the Shabd in us, we experience a radical change in our approach to life. We quite naturally adjust our priorities and make the effort to behave in a way that is in harmony with who we are and with the world. Our problems don't go away, but we are stronger and better equipped to deal with them. We don't lose our balance and we maintain our inner peace.

The peace we find through meditation is independent of any external factor. In that peace we are aware of reality. Meditation makes us more focused, more skilful and more productive in everything we do. With meditation we give direction to our life, and we purify ourselves. It removes the tensions and the junk that clutter our mind. Meditation stills the mind and resurrects our soul. Meditation makes us aware of the deep love present inside us. It is the only means to know, experience, and go back to God.

Our Limits on Love

Love, the saints teach us, is the most complete and unshakeable force in life. It is love more than anything else that leads us to a balanced and happy life. But until love becomes our dominant quality, our mind and senses will continue to limit its free flow.

The limits of knowledge

Love is another name for the spirit of God, which is a limitless and all-pervading reality. Our awareness of this divine love is limited by the present dominance of our intellect. The intellect can only reason and quantify. It cannot grasp the eternal and immortal, which can be grasped only by the soul. We cannot imagine God, because the reality that is God is beyond the reach of the human mind and intellect. By thinking, we cannot obtain any experience of him, even though we may read hundreds of books or think thousands of thoughts.

It is necessary to accept with our understanding some of the limitations we face when discussing such a grand subject. Stanley White, in *Liberation of the Soul*, discusses the limitations of the mind in understanding God. He says: "Our mind, as science tells us, is a finite entity. This means it has limits. It can only do so much, and then it can do no more. For example, we can multiply figures in our mind without the assistance of paper and pencil, but we can do so only up to a certain point before we become frustrated. We can hear sounds only in specific frequency ranges, although the sound spectrum extends above and below our audible range. We cannot perceive the presence of x-rays, infra-red, or ultra-violet rays, but this does not mean that they do not exist. Rather, it shows that we are unable to verify their existence through the use of our senses.

"At this very moment we are being bombarded by radio waves from our local broadcasting stations, but we cannot verify this existence until we 'tune-in' to their frequency length by means of a specially designed receiver. Few of us would be foolish enough to deny the existence of radio and television transmissions simply because we cannot hear them unaided through our senses. We have thus come across an important principle of life.... There are things which exist that cannot be perceived by the senses.

"...Great religious teachers have said that God is infinite. This means that He is without limitation of any kind. How does a finite entity (the mind) comprehend something infinite like God? It is obvious that we have run into a rather severe problem. How can the mind understand something which is greater than itself?

"...Try to remember as you read that it may not be possible to explain every single concept in detail as there are no words to convey experience which goes beyond the realm of mind and matter....Since words are of the mind, they cannot convey a reality higher than that experienced by the mind. With this point firmly fixed in our awareness, let us now attempt to use words to the best of our ability in an attempt to feed the mind spiritual insights from which it can profit."

Only that knowledge which is utilized in trying to understand God and our true self is, in the final analysis, useful. All other knowledge, although it might be helpful for some aspects of life, is too superficial to help us contact our true self and to realize the power of the Creator within.

We can realize this force by experiencing it, not by reading or by thinking about it. In order to experience it, we need to reach the regions of pure consciousness inside ourselves. By the words 'spiritual life' we mean a life of communion with this force, not a life spent in merely thinking, reading or talking about it.

God is everywhere, in every particle of the creation. He is also present in every one of us, for are we not part of the creation? Typically, as human beings we direct our efforts to finding him outside ourselves. Typically, we never consider searching within. This is an important part of the teachings of the saints, for it gives us a clue as to our error, and where we must search to find him. The principle is simple: The Creator we seek is not to be found outside. The Creator must be realized within the human body.

Once we realize God's power within ourselves, we will break through our limited concepts and find that he is everywhere—there is nowhere in the creation that he is not. Saints tell us that it is not possible to see God in the creation, however, unless we have first experienced him within our own being.

The limits of rituals and ceremonies
Rather than reaching out to God through the ocean of love, we become wrapped up in rituals and traditions. All religions preach the same ethical and spiritual truths for humankind. Their principal teachings are that all people should observe good conduct, have faith in the Creator, love him and attain communion with him.

Instead of emphasizing these fundamental spiritual points, the present-day religions ask us to worship or venerate past mystics such as Christ, Moses, Muhammad, Buddha, Krishna, Lao Tzu, Guru Nanak and so forth. They do not tell us how these mystics attained spiritual eminence or how we can effectively meet them so as to learn from them. They stress the necessity of having faith in one religious scripture or another, but they do not give us details as to how we can have the same spiritual experiences described in them. They tell us that our aim is to attain communion with God but fail to provide us with the tools to do so. They promise salvation, but on faith, and only after death.

Rites and rituals have taken the place of the experience of God. We are content to go to churches, synagogues, mosques and temples on the prescribed holy days, thinking that by attending such services and by listening to a priest, rabbi, mullah or pundit recite our holy scriptures we will gain salvation. But that is only a delusion of the mind.

If our aim is to reunite ourselves with God, how can this be achieved through rituals and ceremonies? Liturgies, rituals, ceremonies and places of worship only limit and hinder our efforts to search within because they put external worship in its place. As the Bible explains, "The kingdom of God is within you" (Luke 17:21); or, as St. Paul puts it, "Know ye not that ye are the temple of God, and that the Spirit of God dwelleth in you?" (2 Cor. 6:16). Most of us are familiar with these words from the Bible. But do we understand them, or take note? It would seem we do not. Actually, our temples, mosques and synagogues stand as statements of how we try to limit God to the physical. How can we limit the Unlimited? How can God, who is everywhere, be constrained by walls of brick and mortar or stone?

Saints point to the truth and speak of a simple path to the divine reality which is inside every person. This path, they say, is a natural way to self-discovery. It has been created by God and has been in existence for as long as human beings have lived. It is not man-made. It has nothing to do with rituals or ceremonies, nor does it end in moral conduct or good works. Saints say that God exists and that all religions try to establish communion with him. The path, or discipline, of communion with God is commonly called religion. 'Religion' comes from the Latin word 'religare' which means 'to bind' or 'to unite'. Its real purpose is hidden in the root of the word. Religion means 're-uniting with

God'. We can reunite ourselves with God only if we find him within. The underlying spiritual path is the same for all. Anyone who remembers God and achieves inner communion may be called God's true devotee, irrespective of who he is.

God created human beings, and only later did they become Christians, Buddhists, Jews, Sikhs, Muslims and so forth. There were no Sikhs five hundred years ago, no Muslims thirteen hundred years ago, no Christians two thousand years ago, no Buddhists two thousand five hundred years ago, and no Jews four thousand years ago. People are people, whether of East or West, and all are equal, as there is a soul in each of them which is a particle of the same Creator.

There is only one God, although in our limitation we call him by different names. For example, to quench his thirst, one person may ask for *water*. A person from a different country may ask for *agua* and another for *pani* but they are all asking for the same H_2O regardless of the name they call it.

To realize God, one may belong to any religion. To attain communion with the Creator, it is not necessary to give up one's own traditional religion. All human beings can meet God within, regardless of their gender, social status or religion.

Saints tell us that though God is to be found inside the temple of the body, between the soul and God lies the curtain of egoism and this is why the soul cannot see God. Both live in the same temple, at the same time, but they do not see each other. No ritual or ceremony can change this fact. Only true spirituality, the practice of inner meditation, can lift the curtain.

The limits of our worship

The real church or temple of God is the human form. This is a simple truth, yet perhaps only one person in a million makes his or her actual search for God within. External worship, the saints say, is not only limited but useless. St. Paul says: "And what agreement hath the temple of God with idols? For ye are the temple of the living God" (2 Cor. 6:16).

If someone were to throw a stone through the window of our church or temple, we might fly after him in a rage and punish him as a temple desecrator—yet God dwells in that very person. Daily we ravage the real temple of God, the human body, by all manner of thoughts, words and actions. We search for God throughout the physical universe, yet fail to recognize where he can be found— within each and every one of us. We foolishly believe that mystics and saints speak only figuratively when they tell us that the Creator is to be found within. We fail to grasp the literal meaning of their words.

We limit our worship of God when we ask him for things as if we were bargaining at a marketplace. Normally, the benefits we expect from him have to do with physical or material things like health, wealth or relationships. If we succeed in getting what we want, we only become more involved in the creation. This type of worship is more like a commercial transaction in which we try to bribe God. If he gives us what we want, we will give so much in charity or we will do such and such a thing. In reality all these limited forms of worship are nothing but 'spiritual materialism'. As far as true spirituality is concerned, they are useless.

Another form of spiritual materialism is when we mistake doing humane works with spirituality. True spiritual teachers are not concerned with changing this world. They know that this world is a learning stage for the soul. Just as there are stages from elementary school to university, so also there are intermediary learning stages in the journey of the soul. This world is one of these stages.

The souls that incarnate in this world have to learn from the subjects that are offered in this school called 'earth'. Human beings throughout time will be exposed to the same subjects. These subjects present themselves as pairs of opposites. We will always have to deal with feelings of love and hatred, lust and self-control, greed and contentment, anger and forgiveness, sickness and health, life and death, and so on. This duality is the nature of the world. As long as there are days, there will be nights. As long as there is wealth, there will be poverty. As long as there is war, there will be peace. Our aim should be to graduate from this school by raising ourselves above the pairs of opposites. It is then that we will arrive at our real spiritual home.

If we do not know how to swim, how can we save somebody who is drowning? Would it be selfish to first concentrate our efforts on learning how to swim? Only then can we help those who are drowning. It is very easy to criticize the state of the world, but if each one of us becomes a better person, we will make a far better contribution to improving it than engaging in endless discussions on what everyone else is doing wrong.

Building hospitals, churches, hospices and schools, and doing other types of charitable work—like working with the sick, the dying and the needy—are all worthy humanitarian endeavours and do indeed give us a sense of fulfilment. The trouble is that humanitarianism is mistaken for spirituality. Such activities on their own cannot lead us to God. Unless a person consciously goes inwards, expands his or her own consciousness, has communion with God and becomes like him, all outward efforts—no matter how noble—will be of no avail.

The different religions encourage us to do charitable works, to pray and to live a moral life. They consider these actions the be-all and end-all of religion. Though these actions are very good, they are not enough, because they cannot take us past the lower heavens of the spiritual regions. Once the merits earned for such good behaviour end, the soul has to return to this plane of consciousness and start all over again, because the heavens where we go to be rewarded for our good deeds are all within the domain of the mind. It is in reference to this complexity of the spiritual planes that

Christ says: "In my Father's house there are many mansions" (John 14:2).

Our communication with God is limited when we pray to him with set prayers. If God has the power to grant our wishes, surely he must also have the power to know what we need. It is our own lack of faith which prompts us to beg from him as if he did not know what we need. When we use set prayers, aren't we stopping ourselves from freely expressing our love? Do we need set words to speak to our loved ones? Is God so hard of hearing that we need to repeat our prayers over and over again? Do we worship him out of fear of what he might do to us? Or do we worship him out of vested interests to get what we desire? Either way, prayer motivated by fear or vested interests is very limited. We should worship God only out of love. Rabia Basri, a woman saint of Persia, said: "I wish that I could flood the gates of hell so that no one would worship thee out of fear, and I wish that I could set fire to the gates of paradise so that no one would worship thee for the promises of heaven. Then, everyone would worship thee out of love alone."

Breaking through our limits on love

Love itself is what dissolves all the boundaries and limits we impose on life. Love is the most powerful force in the creation. Without love, life is dry and worthless. Devoid of love a mansion will appear as dreadful as a graveyard. Filled with the light of love, an ill-furnished and dilapidated hut will vibrate with beauty. Love is the richest of all treasures. Without it, there is nothing; and with it, there is everything. As Maharaj Sawan Singh says in *Philosophy of the Masters:*

"Prior to the creation of this world, God was a vast ocean-like All-Consciousness. He was all love, all bliss and self-sufficient. God was everything in Himself and was in a state of blissful quiescence, and His basic form was Love. It was not love for any other being, because none existed. It was for Himself. It was part and parcel of Himself, and He did not have to depend on anything else for this. Such is the indescribable condition of Love."

Love is another name for the spirit of God. The spirit of God is what upholds the universe in balance and harmony. This is why the powerful forces that move in the universe are not in conflict with one another but coexist in perfect balance. If we put ourselves in contact with the spirit of God, we too will enjoy perfect harmony. The same force that upholds the whole creation is also unceasingly supporting and nurturing our own life. That force is love, the positive power of the creation, that includes intelligence, joy and balance. Saints and mystics come to put us in contact with that force so that we may rise above our earthly limitations and rediscover that love in its abundance, balance and joy.

The Camino Real

Speaking about the path of the saints, Dr Johnson writes in the book *With a Great Master in India*: "This path is not a theory. It is not a system of beliefs or dogmas. It is not even a religion, although it embraces all of the values of religion. It is an actual way, a genuine road to be travelled, involving, of course, certain preparation and training as one goes along. In fact, the word 'path' is not altogether appropriate. It is more properly speaking the *Camino Real*, or the King's Highway. It belongs to the royal Masters, and it leads the traveller from earth upward through kingdom after kingdom, from region to region, each one more splendid than the other, in an advancing series until the traveller reaches his final destination, the feet of the supreme Lord of all religions. It is a literal, actual highway, over which the saints and their disciples travel, passing through numberless and vast regions, stopping at different stations en route.

"The passage is really a succession of triumphs, for all the disciples of the saints are enabled to master each region as they enter it, to absorb its knowledge and powers and become citizens of it. The saint is the great captain leading the soul from victory to victory. It is a long and difficult passage, but the saint has been over it many times and he is master of it all. This spiritual journey is, therefore, a long succession of triumphs, until the traveller reaches his grand destination."

The teachings of the saints are a spiritual science where the experiments take place in the laboratory of our own self. To conduct these experiments we need to put our laboratory in order, and put order in our lives. We have to set our priorities straight and act according to them. Our actions need to reflect our intentions. We have to allow time to prove the results for ourselves.

Following a spiritual path

What is it actually that we want from life? What is the purpose of the things we do? Where is the road that we have chosen taking us? Are we really going somewhere or are we running in circles? Are we happy with our lives?

If we are not satisfied with our answers to these questions, we might want to look for a path with a heart, a path in which we can live in the world and at the same time develop what is best in us.

If we have the determination to develop our life to its full potential, we should deepen our spirituality. How are we to do this? What practical steps help deepen our spirituality? We begin first by examining spiritual teachings and being selective about the company we keep. Good company and honest effort will turn us in the direction of God. It is for this reason that every saint stresses to his disciples the importance of good company. It is a fact of human nature that we become like that which we love. A person is influenced by the company he or she keeps. In the company of greedy and lustful persons, we become greedy and lustful. In the company of spiritually inclined people, we too become spiritually inclined. In the company of worldly minded people, we are more likely to become worldly and restless, while in association with spiritual people, we are more likely to become peaceful and serene.

We can also help ourselves by reading spiritual books or by attending meetings where the teachings of the saints are expounded. We may have to do more research, investigating many paths to make sure which one is right for us, which one we feel comfortable with.

It is important to do thorough research to find out which is the best path for us. If with something as trivial as buying a shirt we consider so many before choosing one, how much more careful we should be in making this important decision!

There are many paths and many different teachers. Each one fulfils a particular purpose. If what we are seeking is a path to better our financial situation, to give us more energy, to improve our sex life, to calm the mind, to improve our relationships, to become healthier or to make better business decisions, there are many teachers who can guide us on these paths without our having to go through the hardships and commitment that the teachings of the saints require. The path of the saints is only concerned with self-realization and ultimately with God-realization.

If we decide, after careful consideration, that the teachings of the saints is the right path for us, then we should try for a period of at least one year to abstain from drugs and alcohol, and to follow the vegetarian diet. We should lead an honest and moral life, to see if we will be able to follow this path for the rest of our life.

This path is not a hobby, a club, a religion or a sect. In it there is no pledge to a particular group. No fees are charged. There are no dogmas, no rituals, no ceremonies, no priests, no sacred buildings, no holy scriptures, no group meditation. No blind faith is required. One can belong to any religion and still follow the teachings of the saints.

This path of spirituality involves a personal relationship between the disciple and the spiritual teacher. The teacher asks only for self-commitment to maintain a vegetarian diet, to abstain from drugs and alcohol, to lead a moral life, and to meditate for two and a half hours every day.

This is a path for sober and mature people. When a person is twenty-four years of age or older, he or she can apply for initiation into this path of spirituality. At this age one is less impressionable than in younger years. One has seen enough of the world to know what it has to offer, and one is mature enough to decide whether or not one will be able to take to this path as a way of life.

Perfect balance, lightness of being

We have a responsibility to ourselves. We have to take good care of ourselves. No one else will walk our path for us. We have to walk it ourselves. The spiritual teacher will help us, but we must put in the effort. We can rely on the five pillars of spirituality to give us a strong foundation from which we can build our spiritual life. When we make the resolution to become better human beings, in that very moment we begin to develop our spiritual nature, and, with it, what is best in us. If we are to grow, we have to begin by first bringing the values of spirituality into our material world. We need to step out of the small circle to which we have confined ourselves and to expand our horizon of understanding and action.

Developing peace of mind and stability by relying on the five pillars of spirituality, we will relish the tension-free, stable and joyful state of being that will ensue. Cultivating our spiritual nature and relishing it, our mind will seek to retain this new, more enjoyable way of being and will develop the conviction and determination to obtain, as often as possible, the bliss it has tasted. The more our spiritual nature predominates, the more content and free we become.

When we start to walk on the spiritual path, the downward tendencies of the mind will be gradually destroyed. If we tread the path with conviction, our attitude to life will change and we will become spiritually strong. The upward tendencies of our mind will then be free to bring out all that is best in us.

When we have established ourselves on the way of the saints, we begin to act with balance and equanimity, while within we enjoy the most wonderful peace, joy and lightness of being. Then God-realization becomes a real possibility.

Addresses for Information and Books

INDIAN SUB-CONTINENT

INDIA
The Secretary
Radha Soami Satsang Beas
Dera Baba Jaimal Singh
District Amritsar, Punjab 143204

NEPAL
Mr. Dal Bahadur Shreshta
Radha Soami Satsang Beas
P. O. Box 1646
Gongabu, Dhapasi
Kathmandu
☏+97-1-435-7765

PAKISTAN
Mr. Sadrang Seetal Das
Lahori Mohala, Larkana
Sindh

SRI LANKA
Mr. Chandroo Mirpuri
39/3 Horton Place, Colombo 7

SOUTHEAST ASIA

FOR FAR EAST
Mrs. Cami Moss
RSSB-HK, T.S.T.,
P.O. Box 90745
Kowloon, Hong Kong
☏+852-2369-0625

MALAYSIA
Mr. Selvarajoo Pragasam
No. 15 Jalan SL 10/4
Bandar Sungai Long, Selangor
43000 Kajang

THAILAND
Mr. Harmahinder Singh Sethi
Radha Soami Satsang Beas
58/32 Rachdapitsek Road, Soi 16
Thapra, Bangkok Yai, Bangkok 10600
☏+66-2-868-2186 / 2187

INDONESIA
Mr. Ramesh Sadarangani
Jalan Pasir Putih IV/16, Block E 4
Ancol Timur, Jakarta
DKI Jakarta 14430

PHILIPPINES
Mr. Kay Sham
Science of the Soul Study Centre
9001 Don Jesus Boulevard
Alabang Hills, Cupang
Muntinlupa City, 1771
☏+63-2-772-0111 / 0555

SINGAPORE
Mrs. Asha Melwani
Radha Soami Satsang Beas
19 Amber Road, Singapore 439868
☏+65-6447-4956

ASIA PACIFIC

AUSTRALIA
Mr. Pradeep Raniga
P.O. Box 642
Balwyn North, Victoria 3104

NEW ZEALAND
Mr. Tony Waddicor
Science of the Soul Study Centre
P. O. Box 5331, Auckland
☏+64-9-624-2202

GUAM
Mrs. Hoori M. Sadhwani
115 Alupang Cove
241 Condo Lane, Tamuning 96911

HONG KONG
Mr. Manoj Sabnani
Radha Soami Satsang Beas
3rd Floor, Eader Centre
39-41 Hankow Road
Tsimshatsui, Kowloon
☏+852-2369-0625

76

JAPAN
Mr. Jani G. Mohinani
Radha Soami Satsang Beas
1-2-18 Nakajima-Dori
Aotani, Chuo-Ku, Kobe 651-0052
☎+81-78-222-5353

TAIWAN, R.O.C.
Mr. Haresh Buxani
Science of the Soul Study Group
Aetna Tower Office, 15F., No. 27-9
Sec.2, Jhongjheng E.Rd.
Danshuei Township, Taipei 25170
☎+886-2-8809-5223

NORTH AMERICA

CANADA
Mr. John Abel
#701-1012 Beach Avenue
Vancouver, B.C. V6E 1T7

Science of the Soul Study Centre
2934 -176th Street
Surrey, B.C. V3S 9V4
☎+1-604-541-4792

Mrs. Meena Khanna
149 Elton Park Road
Oakville, Ontario L6J 4C2

MEXICO
Mr. Jorge Villaseñor
Av. De Las Amapolas #39
Condominio Rancho Contento
Zapopan, Jalisco, C.P. 45010

UNITED STATES
Mr. Hank Muller
20038 Indigo Lake Drive
Magnolia, TX 77355

Dr. Vincent P. Savarese
2550 Pequeno Circle
Palm Springs
CA 92264-9522

Dr. Frank E. Vogel
275 Cutts Road
Newport, NH 03773

Dr. Douglas Torr
P.O. Box 2360, Southern Pines
NC 28388-2360

Science of the Soul Study Centre
4115 Gillespie Street
Fayetteville, NC 28306-9053
☎+1-910-426-5306

Science of the Soul Study Centre
2415 East Washington Street
Petaluma, CA 94954-9274
☎+1-707-762-5082

CARIBBEAN

FOR CARIBBEAN
Mr. Sean Finnigan
R.S.S.B. Foundation
P. O. Box 978, Phillipsburg
St. Maarten, N. A.
☎+599-547-0066

BARBADOS, W.I.
Mrs. Jaya Sabnani
1 Sunset Drive South
Fort George Heights
St. Michael BB111 02

CURACAO, N.A.
Mrs. Reshma Jethmalani
Science of the Soul Study Centre
Kaya Seru di Milon 6-9
Santa Catharina
☎+599-9-747-0226

GRENADA, W.I.
Mr. Prakash Amarnani
P.O. Box 726, St. Georges

GUYANA
Mrs. Indu Lalwani
115, Garnette Street
Newtown Kitty, Georgetown

HAITI, W.I.
Mrs. Mousson Finnigan
P.O. Box 2314
Port-au-Prince

JAMAICA, W.I.
Mrs. Reshma Daswani
17 Colombus Height
First Phase, Ocho Rios

ST. MAARTEN, N.A.
Mr. Haresh Balani
R.S.S.B. Foundation
P. O. Box 978
Phillipsburg
☎+599-547-0066

ST. THOMAS
Mrs. Hema Melwani
P.O. Box 600145
USVI-VI00801-6145

SURINAME
Mr. Chandru Samtani
15 Venus Straat
Paramaribo

TRINIDAD, W.I.
Mr. Chandru Chatlani
20 Admiral Court
Westmoorings-by-Sea, Westmoorings

FOR CENTRAL & SOUTH AMERICA

Mr. Hiro W. Balani
Paseo De Farola, 3, Piso 6
Edificio Marina, Malaga, Spain 29016

CENTRAL AMERICA

BELIZE
Mrs. Milan Bhindu Hotchandani
5789 Goldson Avenue, Belize City

PANAMA
Mr. Ashok Tikamdas Dinani
P.O. Box 0302, 00830 Colon

SOUTH AMERICA

ARGENTINA
Mrs. Estela M.I.
Calle Guemes 249, Acassuso
Buenos Aires 1641

BRAZIL
Mr. Guillerme Almeida
SQN 315, Bloco C, Apto. 306 Brasilia
DF 70-774-030

CHILE
Mr. Vijay Harjani
Pasaje Cuatro No. 3438
Sector Chipana, Iquique

COLOMBIA
Mrs. Emma Orozco
Calle 45, #99-25, Medellin 49744

ECUADOR
Dr. Fernando Flores Villalva
Radha Soami Satsang Beas
Calle Marquez de Varela
OE 3-68y Avda. America
P.O. Box 17-21-115, Quito
☎+5932-2-555-988

PERU
Mr. Carlos Fitts
P.O. Box 18-0658
Lima 18

VENEZUELA
Mrs. Helen Paquin
Radha Soami Satsang Beas
Av. Los Samanes con
Av. Los Naranjos Conj
Res. Florida 335
La Florida, Caracas 1012

EUROPE

AUSTRIA
Mr. Hansjorg Hammerer
Sezenweingasse 10, A-5020 Salzburg

BELGIUM
Mr. Piet J. E. Vosters
Driezenstraat 26, Turnhout 2300

BULGARIA
Mr. Deyan Stoyanov
Foundation Radha Soami Satsang Beas
P. O. Box 39, 8000 Bourgas

CYPRUS
Mr. Heraclis Achilleos
P. O. Box 29077, 1035 Nicosia

CZECH REPUBLIC
Mr. Vladimir Skalsky
Maratkova 916, 142 00 Praha 412

DENMARK
Mr. Tony Sharma
Sven Dalsgaardsvej 33, DK-7430 Ikast

FINLAND
Ms. Anneli Wingfield
P. O. Box 1422, 00101 Helsinki

FRANCE
Mr. Pierre de Proyart
7 Quai Voltaire, Paris 75007

GERMANY
Mr. Rudolf Walberg
P. O. Box 1544, D-65800 Bad Soden

GIBRALTAR
Mr. Sunder Mahtani
RSSB Charitable Trust Gibraltar
15 Rosia Road
☎+350-412-67

GREECE
Mr. Themistoclis Gianopoulos
6 Platonos Str. 17672 Kallithea, Attiki

ITALY
Mrs. Wilma Salvatori Torri
Via Bacchiglione 3, 00199 Rome

**THE NETHERLANDS
(HOLLAND)**
Mr. Henk Keuning
Kleizuwe2, Vreeland 3633AE

Radha Soami Satsang Beas
Middenweg 145 E
1394 AH Nederhorst den Berg
☎+31-294-255-255

NORWAY
Mr. Manoj Kaushal
Langretta 8
N-1279 Oslo

POLAND
Mr. Vinod Sharma
Ul. 1go Sierpnia 36 B, M-100
PL-02-134 Warsaw

PORTUGAL
Mrs. Sharda Lodhia
Torres das Palmeiras, Lote 68, 11° C,
2780-145 Oeiras

ROMANIA
Mrs. Carmen Cismas
C.P. 6-12, 810600 Braila

SLOVENIA
Mr. Marko Bedina
Brezje pri Trzicu 68, 4290 Trzic

SPAIN
Mr. J. W. Balani
Fundacion Cultural RSSB
Fca Loma del Valle S/N
Cruce de Penon de Zapata
Alhaurin De la Torre, Malaga 29130
☎+34-952-414-679

SWEDEN
Mr. Lennart Zachen
Norra Sonnarpsvägen 29
SE-286 72 Asljunga

SWITZERLAND
Mr. Sebastian Züst
Weissenrainstrasse 48
CH 8707 Uetikon am See

UNITED KINGDOM
Mr. Narinder Singh Johal
Haynes Park, Haynes
MK45 3BL Bedford
☎+44-1234-381-234

AFRICA

BENIN
Mr. Jaikumar T. Vaswani
01 Boite Postale 951
Atlantique, Cotonou 01

BOTSWANA
Dr. Krishan Lal Bhateja
P. O. Box 402539, Gaborone

CONGO
Mr. Prahlad Parbhu
143 Kasai Ave. Lubumbashi

GHANA
Mr. Murli Chatani
Radha Soami Satsang Beas
P. O. Box 3976, Accra
☎+233-242-057-309

IVORY COAST
Mr. Konan N'Dri
Boite Postale 569, Abidjan 08

KENYA
Mr. Surinder Singh Ghir
35 Mutty Court
(Kipepu RD), Nairobi

LESOTHO
Mr. Sello Wilson Moseme
P. O. Box 750, Leribe 300

LIBYA (G.S.P.L.A.J.)
Mr. Roshan Lal
P.O. Box 38930, Bani Walid

MADAGASCAR
Mr. Francis Murat
Lote 126B, Ambohiminono
Antanetibe, Antananarivo 101

MAURITIUS
Dr. I. Fagoonee
17 Manick Avenue
La Louise, Quatre Bornes

NAMIBIA
Mrs. Jennifer Carvill
P. O. Box 449
Swakopmund 9000

NIGERIA
Mr. Nanik N. Balani
G.P.O. Box 5054, Marina, Lagos

RÉUNION
Ms. Marie-Lynn Marcel
5 Chemin 'Gonneau, Bernica
St Gillesles Hauts 97435

SIERRA LEONE
Mr. Kishore S. Mahboobani
82/88 Kissy Dock Yard
P. O. Box 369, Freetown

SOUTH AFRICA
Mr. Gordon Clive Wilson
P. O. Box 47182, Greyville 4023

Radha Soami Satsang Beas
P.O. Box 5270, Cresta 2118
☎+27-11-792-7644

SWAZILAND
Mr. Peter Dunseith
P. O. Box 423, Mbabane

TANZANIA
Mr. D.N. Pandit
P.O. Box 1963, Dar-Es-Salaam

UGANDA
Mr. Sylvester Kakooza
Radha Soami Satsang Beas
P. O. Box 31381
Kampala

ZAMBIA
Mr. Chrispin Lwali
P.O. Box 12094
Nchanga North Township
Chingola

ZIMBABWE
Mr. G.D. Wright
Pharmanova, P. O. Box 1726
Harare

MIDDLE EAST

BAHRAIN
Mr. Mangat Rai Rudra
Flat No. 12, Building No. 645
Road No. 2107
Manama 321

ISRAEL
Mr. Michael Yaniv
Moshav Sde Nitzan 59
D.N. Hanegev 85470

KUWAIT
Mr. Vijay Kumar
Yousef AL Badar Street Salmiya
Block 10, Flat #8, Bldg 28

U.A.E.
Mr. Daleep Jatwani
Radha Soami Services Centre
P.O. Box 37816, Dubai
☎+971-4-339-4773

Books on This Science

SOAMI JI MAHARAJ
Sar Bachan Prose (*The Yoga of the Sound Current*)
Sar Bachan Poetry (*Selections*)

BABA JAIMAL SINGH
Spiritual Letters

MAHARAJ SAWAN SINGH
The Dawn of Light
Discourses on Sant Mat
My Submission
Philosophy of the Masters, in 5 volumes
Spiritual Gems
Tales of the Mystic East

MAHARAJ JAGAT SINGH
The Science of the Soul
Discourses on Sant Mat, Volume II

MAHARAJ CHARAN SINGH
Die to Live
Divine Light
Light on Saint John
Light on Saint Matthew
Light on Sant Mat
The Master Answers
The Path
Quest for Light
Spiritual Discourses, in 2 volumes
Spiritual Heritage
Thus Saith the Master

BOOKS ABOUT THE MASTERS
Call of the Great Master—Daryai Lal Kapur
Heaven on Earth—Daryai Lal Kapur
Treasure Beyond Measure—Shanti Sethi
With a Great Master in India—Julian P. Johnson
With the Three Masters, in 3 volumes—Rai Sahib Munshi Ram

INTRODUCTION TO SPIRITUALITY
A Spiritual Primer—Hector Esponda Dubin
Honest Living—M. F. Singh

The Inner Voice—C. W. Sanders
Liberation of the Soul—J. Stanley White
Life is Fair: The Law of Cause and Effect—Brian Hines

BOOKS ON MYSTICISM
A Treasury of Mystic Terms, Part I: The Principles of Mysticism
    (6 volumes)—John Davidson
The Holy Name: Mysticism in Judaism—Miriam Caravella
Yoga and the Bible—Joseph Leeming

BOOKS ON SANT MAT IN GENERAL
In Search of the Way—Flora E. Wood
Living Meditation: A Journey beyond Body and Mind
    —Hector Esponda Dubin
Message Divine—Shanti Sethi
The Mystic Philosophy of Sant Mat—Peter Fripp
Mysticism: The Spiritual Path, in 2 volumes—Lekh Raj Puri
The Path of the Masters—Julian P. Johnson
Radha Soami Teachings—Lekh Raj Puri

MYSTICS OF THE EAST SERIES
Bulleh Shah—J. R. Puri and T.R. Shangari
Dadu: The Compassionate Mystic—K. N. Upadhyaya
Dariya Sahib: Saint of Bihar—K. N. Upadhyaya
Guru Nanak: His Mystic Teachings—J. R. Puri
Guru Ravidas: The Philosopher's Stone—K. N. Upadhyaya
Kabir: The Great Mystic—Isaac A. Ezekiel
Kabir: The Weaver of God's Name—V. K. Sethi
Mira: The Divine Lover—V. K. Sethi
Saint Namdev—J. R. Puri and V. K. Sethi
Saint Paltu: His life and teachings—Isaac A. Ezekiel
Sarmad: Martyr to Love Divine—Isaac A. Ezekiel
Sultan Bahu—J. R. Puri and K. S. Khak
Tukaram: The Ceaseless Song of Devotion—C. Rajwade
Tulsi Sahib: Saint of Hathras—J. R. Puri and V. K. Sethi

BOOKS FOR CHILDREN
The Journey of the Soul—Victoria Jones

For Internet orders, please visit: **www.rssb.org**

For book orders <u>within</u> India, please write to:

Radha Soami Satsang Beas
BAV Distribution Centre, 5 Guru Ravi Dass Marg
Pusa Road, New Delhi 110005